Intimacy

Intimacy

An International Survey of the Sex Lives of People at Work

Andrew Kakabadse
Cranfield School of Management, UK

and

Nada K. Kakabadse
Northampton Business School, UK

First published 2004 by
PALGRAVE MACMILLAN
Houndmills, Basingstoke, Hampshire RG21 6XS and
175 Fifth Avenue, New York, N. Y. 10010
Companies and representatives throughout the world

PALGRAVE MACMILLAN is the global academic imprint of the Palgrave Macmillan division of St. Martin's Press, LLC and of Palgrave Macmillan Ltd. Macmillan® is a registered trademark in the United States, United Kingdom and other countries. Palgrave is a registered trademark in the European Union and other countries.

ISBN 1–4039–4324–9

This book is printed on paper suitable for recycling and made from fully managed and sustained forest sources.

A catalogue record for this book is available from the British Library.

Library of Congress Cataloging-in-Publication Data
Kakabadse, Andrew.
   Intimacy : an international survey of the sex lives of people at work / Andrew Kakabadse and Nada K. Kakabadse.
      p. cm.
   Includes bibliographical references and index.
   ISBN 1–4039–4324–9 (cloth)
      1. Sex in the workplace. I. Title: International survey of the sex lives of people at work. II. Kakabadse, Nada. III. Title.
HF5549.5.S45K34 2004
306.7–dc22   2004042096

10   9   8   7   6   5   4   3   2   1
13   12   11   10   09   08   07   06   05   04

Printed and bound in Great Britain by
Antony Rowe Ltd, Chippenham and Eastbourne

Contents

List of Tables   vi

List of Figures   vii

List of Cases   viii

Acknowledgement   x

Chapter 1   Introduction   1

Chapter 2   What We Know So Far   7
Sexuality and Religion   14
Intimacy at Work   20
  'Appropriate' Workplace Behaviour   23
  Harassment   25
  Intimacy   28
Barriers and Consequences   37
  What More To Know?   42

Chapter 3   The Study   43
Demographics   44
Intimacy: Nature and Context   47
Nature of Relationships at Work   57
Intimacy Outcomes and Impact   69
  Those Directly Involved   69
  Third Party Involvement   79
IT Revolution   86
Management Intervention   91
Company Policy   98

Chapter 4   Addressing Intimacy   111

References   127

Index   137

List of Tables

Table 2.1	Generations Values Outlook	37
Table 2.2	Organisational Policies Regarding Workplace Romance	41
Table 3.1	Marital Status	44
Table 3.2	Role Within the Organisation	44
Table 3.3	Years in the Organisation	45
Table 3.4	Size – Number of Employees in the Organisation	45
Table 3.5	Sector	46
Table 3.6	Length of Working Week	46
Table 3.7	Perception of Organisational Culture	52
Table 3.8	Job Satisfaction	57
Table 3.9	Experience of Intimacy	65
Table 3.10	Intimacy Impact on Group and Organisation Effectiveness	76
Table 3.11	IT Impact on Intimacy Experience	86
Table 3.12	Existence of Diversity Policy	101
Table 4.1	Approaches to Addressing Intimacy Encounters	113
Table 4.2	Advice on Intimacy	116

List of Figures

Figure 2.1   Loving Relationships   30
Figure 3.1   Types of Workplace Intimacy   47
Figure 3.2   Values and Relationships   53
Figure 3.3   Attitudes Towards Relationships at Work   57
Figure 3.4   Reasons for the Development of Relationships
              in the Workplace   64
Figure 3.5   Intimacy Experience; With Whom?   67
Figure 3.6   Personal Status   68
Figure 3.7   Inhibitors to Relationship(s) in the
              Workplace   69
Figure 3.8   Outcome of Intimate Relationship(s)   70
Figure 3.9   Impact of Other Peoples' Relationships   79
Figure 3.10   Affect of Intimate Relationship on Self   80
Figure 3.11   Management's Reaction to Intimacy
              Relationships   94
Figure 3.12   Policy Recommendations Towards Physical
              Intimacy   104
Figure 4.1   Intimacy   119

List of Cases

Case 1   The Prof, the Student and Some 'hanky panky'   7
Case 2   Intimacy, Support and Improvement   48
Case 3   The Journalist, the Friend and the Divine   49
Case 4   Feeling Ethical And Still Breaking My Rules   55
Case 5   Not For Me   58
Case 6   Not To Be Lonely   58
Case 7   The Man of Intellect Who Taught Me That I
            Had a Heart   59
Case 8   Penny Dropped Much Later   63
Case 9   Clever, Attractive and in Service   65
Case 10   Divorced, Dating and Delectable   66
Case 11   The 'Fly by Night' Who Taught Me About
            Courage   71
Case 12   Recollections of a Gay Man   75
Case 13   Pretending for Social Events   78
Case 14   Intimacy in the Military   80
Case 15   Going Dutch   83
Case 16   My Problem is Zippergate   85
Case 17   The Paradox of a Virtual Relationship – Trust
            or Treachery?   87
Case 18   Too Shy to Speak   92
Case 19   Too Sensitive To Handle   96
Case 20   April's Tale   99
Case 21   No Policies To Speak Of   101
Case 22   The Grey Area of Office Behaviour: A Canadian
            Perspective   106
Case 23   From Special Friendship To Harassment   108
Case 24   Rational About You Lot; Limbic About Myself   109
Case 25   Dentistry: Aussie Style   118
Case 26   I Am A People's Person   121
Case 27   When Realised?   121
Case 28   Sharing   122
Case 29   Do Not Expect a Lot of Change   122
Case 30   The Cross I Bear   123

Case 31   Trapping Your Boss   123
Case 32   Overstep The Mark And It All Goes Wrong   124
Case 33   It Was Left Up To Me   125

Acknowledgement

Particular and grateful thanks are offered to Andrew Myers for his statistical wizardry, to Sheena Darby for her patience in typing draft after draft and also for her critical, editorial eye. Our gratitude also to Dr Stephen Swailes for his comments and suggestions and to our colleagues who conducted in depth interviews with some of the study participants.

We also thank all of those who took part in the research outlined in this report. Without the sharing of your experiences, your candidness and your judgement concerning a particularly delicate and fundamental aspect of all of our lives, namely our most intimate of relationships, this study would never have taken place.

We are indebted to you all.

1
Introduction

This report outlines the results of an extensive international survey into a delicate area of human interaction, namely, the intimate and at times, not so private side to sexual conduct in the workplace.

This survey was partly inspired through witnessing the distress of a colleague involved in an intimacy encounter. We, the authors, could do little to assist, partly because the colleague was employed at another university on the east coast of the USA, but also because the situation had 'gone too far'. The colleague's circumstances are described in Case 1 (Chapter 2). Briefly, he (the colleague) had the 'misfortune' to fall in love with his doctoral student, who was a female in her early thirties. That relationship survived. A number of those who took the moral high ground, condemning this affair, have seen their personal circumstances deteriorate resulting in divorce and family disruption. In our eyes, the colleague in question did little wrong except to be disliked, be unpopular and also exhibit that 'human failing' of falling in love with the supposedly wrong person.

The other reason for pursuing this research was the reaction of others in the workplace to our colleague's plight. Most publicly disapproved of him but did nothing to damage his career or image. In private, some even felt 'sorry' for him. Still, others recognised that they too could have been at the centre of such unwelcome attention. The reaction of many in that university was anxiety, 'There by the grace of God go I', was a comment made by more than one senior colleague. On noticing the discomfort of so many, it was Nada who suggested that a study be undertaken exploring the topic of workplace intimacy and the nature, if any, of sexual conduct at work. Andrew poo-pooed the idea.

'I don't think anyone will talk to you. It is too sensitive and private', said Andrew.

Nada persisted and began with just four interviews. What should have been hour long discussions turned into three to four hour marathons. People were only too willing to share their personal concerns. In fact, in the next 'crop of interviews', certain individuals expressed disappointment at not being invited to be interviewed. Similar to before, hour long sessions extended into three to four hour 'therapy sessions'. Those interviewed were managers, professionals, secretaries and other support staff. The unburdening of personal intimate relationship concerns and how these deeply impacted on work life were consistent themes throughout the interviews. As it turned out, individuals from all walks of life, social status, wealth and background participated in this most sensitive voyage of personal intimate discovery.

All those who participated took the discussions seriously. The relationship challenges people faced and the concerns they expressed were deeply felt. There was little frivolity although occasionally humour did surface. One interviewee on being asked whether she had experienced physical intimacy in the workplace responded, 'No! and do you know why? Nobody ever asked but I wish they had!'.

And so we embarked on a serious study of the two most fundamental aspects of human beings, that of people's private, intimate, and for many, sexual life and the challenges individuals face in their workplace.

The seriousness of this survey is highlighted in two particular ways. First, the depth of the literature review which traces intimacy and its impact on the conduct of life back to the times of the Old Testament, through the Greek and Roman eras, through medieval times and the industrial revolution to our world of today. What the literature review clearly shows is that intimacy and sexual conduct at work has not been seen as a 'cheap' personal 'thrill' or idiosyncrasy, but more as a serious and profound concern. Interestingly, intimacy and religion have been historically intertwined and recognised as a profound influence on the moulding of whole societies. Pleasure and procreation examined through the lenses of the different faiths of this world, position sexuality as a distinct force in the shaping of the philosophies underlying the pursuit of life. Noteworthy are the differences of interpretation and levels of importance attributed to sexuality across varying religions.

Second, the study itself. Interviews were undertaken exploring people's experiences of intimacy. As highlighted, the interviews were lengthy, exploring not only the 'racy' bits directly related to intimacy encounters, but also scrutinised people's attitudes, their ethics and their frustrations. Attention was given to understanding the dynamics surrounding people's jobs and the influence and impact of the organisation on each person. The learning from the interviews was captured through the drafting of an extensive questionnaire. Much attention was given to designing the questionnaire to allow for in depth analysis of the relationships between desire and realisation, opportunity and frustration, choice and reconsideration. Although intimacy is a personal experience, the opportunity for, or discouragement of, intimate experiences in the workplace were examined at the broader enterprise level. Therefore, in this report, analysis and discussion extends from the individual and their job to the culture of organisation, to the nature of management intervention when intimacy takes on a physical dimension and to the corporate guidelines and policies scoping personal and professional conduct in the workplace.

More specifically, Chapter 2 provides an overview of the literature. Analysis of intimacy amongst public figures is interwoven with an updating of the policies towards sexual conduct in the workplace of key private sector and public service organisations. Why we react to intimacy in the ways that we do is addressed through a historical analysis of sexuality and religion, highlighting how the influence of paganism is still visible today. One particular point is emphasised, namely, that until recent times, the divide between work and private life was hazy. Agrarian communities, shaped as family and village structures, were configured according to the daily demands and fluctuations of the seasons, thus leaving little room for distinction to be drawn between what is my private life and what is work. However, with the advent of organised markets and the subdivision of labour, attitudes changed. The emergence of specialisation and the influence of market forces raised sharp distinctions between work and home, particularly accentuated in the industrial revolution. From the industrial revolution to the information revolution (present day), the debate has changed again with discussion now of appropriate workplace behaviour being interwoven with love and intimacy, whilst attempting to draw distinction between intimacy and harassment. In fact, sexual harassment is identified as a potent perspective of intimacy in today's private and public service enterprises. From such analysis, Chapter 2 concludes by questioning whether the work/private life divide will continue. Somewhat in parallel with medieval times, the information revolution has been a powerful force in blurring the work/home boundaries. With an increasing number of people utilising the computer as their office, working from home is becoming increasingly commonplace. Further, the two emerging generations, commonly known as X and Y, do not consistently display the same work ethic passion as the post World War II baby boomers. Personal development and self satisfaction equally balance against career aspiration and the determination to succeed. However, generations X and Y are also at the receiving end of extensive change, mergers, acquisitions, downsizing and overall maturing of markets. Whatever the ambitions and personal desires of each individual, hanging on to your job is as much today's new reality as 'having a good time'. Whether wanting to or not, needing to spend more time attending at/to work is now commonplace. On this basis, where does one meet new friends and nurture the intimacies fundamental to our lives?

Pursuing the theme of whether personal and professional life today are becoming as inter-mingled as pre-medieval times, Chapter 3 outlines the results of the international intimacy survey we conducted. Well over 200 people of different nationalities, religions, ages, backgrounds and social status, participated in the study. The male/female split is roughly two thirds, one third respectively. Our results highlight that 60 per cent of the survey participants admit to an intimate experience of sorts in the workplace. We did not expect such a level of admission. In order to understand why so many people have entered into intimate encounters, attention is given to understanding a wide range of topics, such as

- people's values and views towards intimacy,
- the quality of their work relationships,
- their levels of job satisfaction,
- culture of organisation,
- the outcome of intimate encounters,
- with whom physical intimacy (sex at work) is experienced,
- the inhibitors to the conduct of intimacy,
- the reaction of the individuals involved and affected third parties to intimacy occurrences,
- how advances in communication technology have provided opportunities (or not) for intimacy experiences,
- the reaction of management, and,
- the overall reaction of the organisation to intimacy encounters in the workplace.

After such an overview, the question remains, what to do? Before attempting to respond to, 'What to do with intimacy at work?',

Chapter 4 starts by questioning what is normality. Certainly the blurring of work and private life has clearly emerged from this survey. What also comes out of this survey is that, in the eyes of many, intimacy at work is basically not a problem, is on the increase (or at least will not go away) and many report improvements in work performance resulting from the exhilaration of intimacy experiences. So, what is the problem that requires treatment and attention? The various options to consider in responding to intimacy circumstances are examined in Chapter 4.

Throughout this text, stories, cameos and case examples of people's experiences and intimacy incidents are provided, hopefully bringing life to the trends identified through the survey. All the cases in this book are real. However, people's names, location and personal circumstances have been changed in an effort to guard their anonymity. Thus, any likeness in terms of names or personal circumstances to any one individual is entirely accidental and unintentional.

Certainly, no clear-cut picture emerges emphasising the difference between right and wrong, or what is appropriate and inappropriate. Further, the level of attention given to sexual harassment in the academic literature and more popularly in the press and media is judged, from this survey, as questionable. The incidence of sexual harassment is reported as occurring even less than sexually consummated gay relationships at work. Of course, sexual harassment is a deeply distressing experience and, when it arises, should rightly be stamped on so that the trauma does not continue or extend to others. It is just that the respondents in this survey suggest that sexual harassment does not occur as much as journalists and academics would have us believe.

Talking to a senior media manager about the results of our survey he reflected,

'What you mean is that people are "bonking" because they want to and basically are not a bother to anyone else!'

'Basically, yes', was our response. But the simplicity of these words hide an emerging morality concerning how people view their work lives in order to pursue their desired, healthy, social life.

What was our motivation, as authors and researchers, in pursuing this research? Well, it is to enhance understanding by capturing trends, stories and views of a particularly complex and relatively unexplored area of working life. We hope, through this report, that we are able to offer insights concerning a profound experience that is likely to come ever more prominent, namely the personal and, in may ways, unique intricacies underlying the working lives of so many of us.

2
What We Know So Far

Case 1   The Prof, the Student and Some 'hanky panky'

A talented, internationally well known, east coast based, US university professor, also chairman of his specialist department, declared to his colleagues his intention to marry his doctoral student. She, an equally talented aspiring academic, just turned 30, admitted that their relationship had been covertly conducted for fear of unwelcome comment and criticism from their colleagues. For the sake of equity, governance and good conduct, on announcing their relationship, the doctoral candidate was assigned a new supervisor so that any conflict of interests would be minimised. However, despite the couple's attempts to pursue organisational propriety, their fears of an emotional outburst were realised. Certain faculty members accused the professor of unethical behaviour and of taking advantage of a student and a woman at that! These criticisms were made despite her age and the fact that she had held positions of considerable managerial responsibility prior to entering the doctoral programme. She was assertive. She displayed considerable confidence. She certainly was no pushover! Yet, despite her impressive aura, the female doctoral candidate equally endured criticism from her own doctoral peers and from the secretaries in the department on the basis of, 'Why did you keep this a secret?'

The professor in question was not a popular figure. His manner was brusque and dismissive. He equally had pushed through policies that were resented but were necessary for the survival of the department. He had become the centre of unwelcome comment long before his relationship with his student became public. His doctoral student partner, who was much more sociable than him, mixed well with most in the department. At lunches and tea breaks, when many of the mature, postgraduate students and secretaries socialised, criticising the professor became common practice. The woman was unfortunately caught between having to listen to their comments concerning her partner and not being able to declare her 'love interest' in the man. Thus, when their relationship came to light, she was considered a 'traitor'. The Dean of the faculty became involved and the so-called 'scandal' became centre stage for the following weeks. Eventually, the

7

situation calmed down, as much due to the professor having made a public apology for his conduct. The female student felt she could only proceed with her doctorate if she changed departments, which she duly did. The couple married and on her successful award of PhD, the two left the university and found employment elsewhere.

Many years on, they are together and have remained happily married. They are also working together as a professional husband and wife team. Some of their original critics have divorced and one has since died. Since that time, certain other couples, working at the same university have declared their interest in each other, have married but have not attracted comparable admonishment as the professor and his student.

What was so scandalous? In 1891, the young, talented, 24 year old, Marie Sklodowska arrived in Paris and began experiments in the laboratory of Pierre Curie, in the School of Physics and Chemistry. Her marriage to her tutor, Pierre in 1895, marked the start of a partnership that was soon to achieve results of world significance with the discovery of polonium and that of radium, for which in 1903, together with Henri Becquerel, they received the Nobel Prize for physics (Ham, 2003). Marie Curie introduced the world to radiation. Yet when the tutor married his student in 1895, there was no outcry or public scandal. At that time no-one knew that Pierre and Marie Curie were to be the founders of the treatment of cancer. They were just two diligent academics, the professor and his student.

In contrast to the long term nature of the professional and personal relationship of the Curies, adultery on a blatant scale has been repeatedly committed by public figures. Some have been castigated and became the hate figures of the day for their 'immorality'! Others, equally in the limelight, were hardly mentioned. The British Prime Minister, William Ewart Gladstone observed in 1868 that of the 13 prime ministers he had known, 11 had been adulterers (Glover, 1998). Gladstone's comments were not far off 'the mark'. The Liberal Prime Minister, Lloyd George, nicknamed the 'Goat', is described by historians as a 'sexual charmer', a man that held a passion for the efficient indulgence of conducting brisk sex on the cabinet table (Arnold-Baker, 1995; Parris, 1998). The late Lord Geoffrey Rippon, was purportedly taking girlfriends to stylish Annabel's (The Sunday Times, 1998). The 1950s Labour Party Leader, Hugh Gaitskell, is reported to have conducted an affair with Anna Fleming (the wife of Ian Fleming and creator of James Bond). Hugh Gaitskell and Anna Fleming were publicly seen together in ballrooms and the finest restaurants (The

Sunday Times, 1998). The former Tory Prime Minister, John Major, admitted his four-year affair with the former Conservative minister, Edwina Currie, after she published her political diary (The Economist, 2002). At the time of the affair, Mrs Currie was a backbencher and Mr Major a whip in the Thatcher government (Currie, 2002). Such episodes came and went without inflicting too much damage to the public figure in question or their constituents.

The saga of Lord Cecil Parkinson, Conservative, UK Secretary of State for Trade and Industry, and his former secretary, Sara Keays, highlights that supposed promises made, that in turn are not honoured, have a high price tag (BBC1, 1983). After considerable media attention, Lord Parkinson resigned his post in 1983 after Ms Keays announced that she was expecting his child (BBC1, 1983).

In contrast to Parkinson, a number of public figures have experienced a happier ending. In British politics, certain MPs have ended up marrying their secretaries or researchers. Robin Cook, the former Foreign Secretary, despite public criticism, married his secretary Gaynor Regan. Other prominent British politicians have pursued a similar path (The Sunday Times, 1998).

American politicians provide an equally colourful present as well as past. One of America's founding fathers, the 3rd US president, Thomas Jefferson, through DNA investigation is concluded to have had illegitimate children by the slave Sally Hemings (Cauchon, 1998). Warren Harding, the 29th Republican President of the United States had fallen in love with 14 year old Miss Nan Britton when he was already married and whilst liaising with another mistress (Parris, 1998). Franklin D. Roosevelt and Eleanor Roosevelt both experienced intimacy outside their marriage (Parris, 1998). Eleanor had a deep emotional affair with journalist, Lorena Hickok, with whom she exchanged approximately 3000 letters. Franklin kept two mistresses, one as his social secretary, Lucy Page Mercer, and the other Marguerite Alice LeHand, nicknamed 'Missy', who lived with him in the White House. President John F. Kennedy is infamous for his string of affairs. Equally infamous is the Bill Clinton and Monica Lewinsky debacle, compounded by the Jennifer Flower allegations that Clinton pursued a love-relationship with her for a considerable number of years.

In continental Europe, the Elysee Palace, France, has witnessed its fair share of French politicians' infidelities. For example, the French journal *Marianne*, reveals the extensive nature of French president's adultery. President Jacques Chirac, similar to his predecessor Francois Mitterrand, is said to have enjoyed a string of love affairs, including one with Italian actress, Claudia Cardinale (Scott, 1998). Valery Giscard d'Estaing, during his presidency, displayed interest in young actresses, allegedly having an affair with Sylvia Kristel, Marlene Jobert as well as Catherine Bokassa, wife of the former emperor of the Central African Republic (Scott, 1998). President François Mitterrand, even when suffering from cancer, is cited to have liaised with women other than his long established mistress, Anne Pingeout, with whom he had an illegitimate daughter (MacIntyre, 1998). In fact, the Swedish journalist, Christina Forsene, in her book, immortalised her affair with socialist president, Mitterrand (Forsne, 1998). Roland Dumas, former foreign minister, is considered to have had an affair with Nahed Ojjeh, the daughter of the Syrian defence and intelligence minister, followed by an affair with Christine Deviers-Jancour, who accompanied him on foreign trips (Scott, 1998). The late Greek Prime Minister, Andreas Papandreou, according to his widow, Mimi Papandreou, conducted an affair with her, engaging in sex acts in his office, whilst still married to his first wife (Giovanni, 1998).

In complete contrast to politicians but similar to Pierre and Marie Curie, certain professionally successful couples started their intimacy within the workplace. Notable is that of Beatrice Potter, who, in 1891, introduced her research into the co-operative movement to Sidney Webb (Nolan, 1988). Beatrice and Sidney became close friends. In 1892 they were married and became a critical driving force behind the Fabian Society. Additionally, Sidney and Beatrice Webb worked on several books together including *The History of Trade Unionism* (1894) and *Industrial Democracy* (1897). Their research and writings convinced them of the need to establish a new political party that was committed to realising socialism through parliamentary election. On 27th February 1900, the Fabian Society joined with the Independent Labour Party, the Social Democratic Federation and trade union leaders to form the Labour Representations Committee (LRC), which put forward 15 candidates in the 1900 election, of which two won seats in the House of Commons (Nolan, 1988).

Not just in political and academic life, but also intimacy in the military has been widely reported. Throughout history, the military has sought to regulate the level of socialising amongst the rank and file, as well as to controlling sex and love engagements within the Armed Services (Bcersuna, 1997). Yet despite such scrutiny, the late 1990s witnessed many publicised sex related scandals on both sides of the Atlantic. Both men and women have been discharged from the services for being found guilty of adulterous relationships or love affairs, some of which have turned into sexual harassment. In the USA, for example, infidelity is, technically, not illegal. However, a 200 year military tradition does not condone sexual activity. Article 134 of the Uniform Code of Military Justice prohibits adultery when it is 'prejudicial to good order and discipline or will bring distress upon the armed forces' (Biema, 1997: 36). In the US military, the fraternisation rules vary from service to service and are allegedly invoked only when charges are brought forward by an injured party, often by one of the aggrieved spouses of the perpetrators (Gibbs, 1997). One encounter which never turned into a public scandal is the well-known war-time relationship between Dwight Eisenhower (Ike), the married, Allied commander and future president of the USA, and the Irish woman, Kay Summersbay, a divorcee. According to Kay's published memoirs, the relationship lasted from the time they met in May 1942, when she was assigned to be his civilian chauffeur, through to her promotion to his secretary and military aide. The relationship was supposedly intensely romantic and caused Eisenhower's wife, Mamie, to have jealous fits. However, the Ike/Kay relationship apparently was never sexually consummated (Summersby, 1976). Mamie, equally, did not make a formal complaint. All this Kay wrote in her memoirs in the 1970s, long after Ike's death, and at the end of her life when she herself was diagnosed with cancer.

According to the US Army 'dating between soldiers of different rank is not harmful, and usually not improper'. With such perspective in mind, the Navy's first mixed carrier to include servicewomen, the U.S.S. Dwight D. Eisenhower, applied a code that couples who confessed their love for each other to their captain would quietly receive new assignments, without any further prosecution (Biema, 1997). The US Air Force, attracting the greater number of female civilians (26 per cent of its recruits are women, whilst only 20 per cent of its members fly planes), has the harshest rules. Although their manual allows that a marriage between an officer and enlisted person is 'not, by itself evidence of misconduct' it reserves the right to take punitive measures 'based on prior fraternisation' (Biema, 1997: 37).

In fact, since the early 1980s, military rules and arrangements have been complicated by the influx of tens of thousands of women into the armed forces. For example, an opinion poll for Gulf War units reported that 64 per cent of Air Force respondents reported sexual activities in their squad (Francke, 1997). Moreover, the number of prosecutions and adultery courts martial in the Air Force has risen from 42 reported cases in 1992 to 67 in 1996 (Gibbs, 1997; Biema, 1997). The public scandal caused by First Lieutenant Kelly

Flinn, the female bomber pilot's affair with an enlisted airman, Marc Zigo, received considerable media attention and ended up with her discharge from the Air Force (Gibbs, 1997).

In the UK, a public scandal in the 1990s prompted the need for updating previous military codes of conduct. The 1997 court-martial of Lieutenant Commander David Bellingham embarrassingly exposed life at sea. This was followed by the discharge of two women Army officers, Lieutenant Joanna Key and Captain Alison Plat from Northern Ireland, after they allegedly had affairs with married officers (Seamarks and Williams, 1998; Sylvester, 1998). Perhaps the most prominent was the affair in 1997, that turned into sexual harassment, between two high-flying military officers, Lieutenant Colonel Keith Pople, a married father of two, and Lieutenant-Commander Karen Pearce, one of the Navy's top women who, at the time of their affair, was going through a divorce from her Royal Marine husband (Farrell, 1998; Seamark and Williams, 1998). Further 'scandal' followed through the demise of Defence Ministry boss Air Chief Marshall Sir Peter Harding, whose career was severely damaged through his affair with Lady Bienvenida Buck, the Spanish wife of a former Tory MP (Seamark and Williams, 1998).

According to a UK, Ministry of Defence (MoD) spokesman, new guidelines are needed to recognise that society has changed since the original revisions of 1993 (Sylvester, 1998). Under the proposed new rules, only affairs within a military organisation will be deemed unacceptable if trust is damaged between men and women who may have to fight alongside each other. Previously, adultery was seen as a loss of integrity. Under the proposed new rules, adultery will not be tolerated due to the potential inefficiencies that can arise particularly during combat (Sylvester, 1998). Although the new code of conduct for service personnel identifies such qualities as loyalty, integrity, honesty and courage as central to military life, 'adulterous' life conducted outside the services is now being deemed as, in itself, immaterial to the operational capability of the Army. These reviewed guidelines will no longer forbid adulterous relationships with civilians, but they do enhance strict rules concerning drugs and alcohol intake, bullying and sexual harassment (Sylvester, 1998).

As with politicians and the military, a variety of responses are identified in the private sector corporate world to intimacy like relationships and sex scandals. A particular fashion company terminated the contract of its chief executive officer after the Board became aware that, at a trade dinner, he was reported as making 'unwelcome' comments and touching women's bottoms as he danced alongside them at a disco (Rosser and Kay, 2000).

Certain organisations take a more liberal view. A spokesman for British Airways has said that long-term romances are commonplace and that pilots often marry air hostesses or 'check-out' staff (Driscoll, 1998). Equally, Pertemps, the recruitment consultants, were paying for staff to join a dating agency with the same 'ease' as they could previously join health care or pensions provisions (Scrivener, 1998).

In contrast, according to one KPMG employee, the company exercises a strict, though unwritten policy, against office romances. In similar tone, BT has warned employees that if they engage in relationships with colleagues, they may be moved to another department (The Guardian, 1998). IBM and Xerox have stated that they would seek to remove any potential for conflict in possible relationships between employees (Welch, 1998). Marks and Spencer, again different, have indicated that the private lives of their employees is their own concern, providing that what they do does not interfere with their working lives (The Guardian, 1998).

With such contrasts of response to office liaisons, how unusual is the case of the US university professor and his doctoral student (Case 1)? Not very, for in a survey conducted in 1998, 42 per cent of Britons reported having adulterous relationships in comparison to 37 per cent of Italians and 22 per cent of Spaniards (Global Sex Survey, 1998). The Centre for Policy Studies suggest that by the year 2020, with present trends, married couples will be in a minority in Britain and that a substantial proportion of people will be living alone. Most women will be single and only 48 per cent will hold the status of 'wife' (Selbourne, 1999). In the late 20th century, women increasingly gained higher education and entered into paid employment. Marriage based on socalled 'social aptness', where man was the sole bread-winner and woman the family raiser, has been replaced with 'emotional aptness', or the modern 'companion marriage', where mutual support and love are the basis for the relationship (Kremer, 1998). The reality however, is that nearly 66 per cent of American and virtually 50 per cent of British couples divorce (Kremer, 1998). Further, in the UK, threequarters of all couples now live together before marriage (The Economist, 1998a).

So why did the professor in Case 1 attract such unwelcome attention? Because of the 'Teflon' factor or, in the professor's case, the lack of it! The popular, in vogue character, that many admire often projects a smooth and comfortable style. Lloyd George, similar to US

President Warren Harding, lied over matters of intimate relationships in order to remain in office. In fact, the Republican National Committee protected Harding by 'paying off' certain of his mistresses (Parris, 1998). Displaying similar 'social graces', Lloyd George was the 1st World War hero, under whom the phrase, 'a land fit for heroes' was coined (Parris, 1998). Lloyd George was both acclaimed and adored by the masses. In contrast, the UK socialist Prime Minister, Harold Wilson, described as 'one of the most innocent of men to have ever inhabited Downing Street', attracted adverse comment, considered as an adulterer, a crook and even a Russian spy (Parris 1998: 20). For a number of reasons, Wilson was disliked and his media image did little to alter that negative perception. Thus the question that emerges is, does the establishment want you to stay or go? If the answer is go, then any scandal is likely to suffice as an excuse for exit, despite apologies, displays of remorse and promises of better conduct in the future. The real 'sin' of the university professor in Case 1, was his unwelcome manner. Similar to the professor, the 40-year affair between Lillian Ross, a *New Yorker* writer, and the *New Yorker's* editor, the married William Shawn, was professionally productive for both (Ross, 1998). Unable to leave his wife Cecille without her consent, Shawn lived with both women, setting up two homes 11 blocks from each other (Ross, 1998). The arrangement lasted until his death in 1992 (Ross, 1998). Shawn is more portrayed as a hero, whilst the university professor (Case 1) as a villain. Strictly speaking, both did little wrong except 'fall in love', but their personal standing amongst their peers was the real difference.

Sexuality and religion

What is clear is that human sexuality has been a topic of interest and intense debate amongst scholars and theologians throughout the centuries. Through defining its meaning, purpose and modus operandi, historical analysis reveals that the manner in which sexuality was addressed by a society reflected that society's level of maturity. The ancient Greeks perceived that the essence of human existence partly depended on the way individuals, and particularly the leaders, engaged in sexual behaviour. According to Plato (Bloom, 1991), temperance, or the mastery of self, was seen as a necessary pre-condition to the leadership and mastery of others. Although sexual indulgence was abundant in ancient Greece and the Greco-Roman era, sexual temperance was expected from those who held the role of leader. The paradox of what we expect from our leaders does not apply to ourselves, is as much alive and healthy today as 3000 years ago.

In many ways history has revered sensuality and sexuality as sacred, divine and natural. Many pagan traditions were sensitive to the 'sacred' meaning of human eroticism and sexuality through recognising and acknowledging primordial biological forces, symbolically, spiritually, and physically (Peterson, 2002). Ancient pagan faiths honour and celebrate the *eroto*-sexual dimensions of human expression, not only as divine, but also as essential and pleasurable. Long before Judaism, Christianity and Islam were established, there existed innumerable love, sex and fertility goddesses, revered as deities of sexual affection, fertility and procreation, notably Artemis/Diana, Aphrodite/Venus/ Freya, Shakti/Kali/Durga/Bhairavi, Ishtar, and others (Monaghan, 1997). In Celtic tradition, May was recognised as the month of sexual freedom. In similar vein, Saxons cast magical 'love' spells and worshipped the natural cycles of female sexuality.

Archaeological evidence in the form of artefacts and religious writings suggests that both in ancient and more modern times, the sexual union between a man and a woman is depicted as most sacred, even possessive of magical power. For example, in Mesopotamian texts, male and female symbols are commonly portrayed as sphinxes, griffins, cherubs or winged human creatures portraying gods or sacred places (Gaster, 1962). In fact the word 'cherub' is believed to be derived from 'karibu' meaning 'intercessor', probably emanating from the winged Sphinx depicted as a four-legged beast possessing a lion's body and a human head and identified with Egypt's 4th Dynasty (Gaster, 1962). Under Egypt's Asiatic empire, or the new kingdom (1560–1140 BC), the sphinx was introduced to Phoenicia, Canaan and Syria, moulded with extended wings in both male and female forms, where sometimes the females displayed a row of breasts on the underside of their bodies (Mettinger, 1995). Later manifestations, such as the ancient Greek Eros and the Roman Cupid, are represented as a naked human form with wings and associated with love and sex (Demisch, 1977). The human form cherub was also adopted by the early Christians often depicted as an angel, a symbol that still appears on Valentine's Day cards.

Ironically, the historical and religious roles of cherubs has been both of guardian of morality as well as facilitator of sexual expression. In the story of the Garden of Eden, Cherubums are described as guarding, or barring, the way to the Tree of Life. Two winged sphinxes also appear in Phoenician and Assyrian art forms, either side of the sacred tree. In the Holy of Holies, King Solomon's temple, which housed the Ark of the Covenant, two golden cherubs, entwined in a sexual embrace, were located on top of the Ark, one male and one female, both of which are described in the Book of Kings and in the Babylonian Talmud (Gafini, 2003). Although the origin of these cherubs has led to disagreement amongst Hebrew scholars, mystic scholars depict these forms as the biblical Hebrew god, Yah-weh and the pagan goddess, Asherea. For Cabbalists and other Hebrew mystics, cherub integration represents the essential underlying force that powers the universe. In the biblical prophecy it is thought 'that the space between the sexually entwined cherubs was the source of prophecy' (Gafini, 2003: 37). The cherubs' presentation of the divine is depicted in the Cabbalistic books of the Bahir and the Zohar (*Magnus opus* of Hebrew mysticism) where the cherub pair is referred to as Malchut or Shechinah (divine feminine) and Tiferet (divine masculine) (Gafini, 2003). Certain Cabbalah scholars suggest that the word 'zohar' is translated into the Greek word 'eros' (Gafini, 2003). Thus, whether conceived of as Yin and Yang as in Taoist thought, or Shiva and Shakti in Hindu mythology, the masculine and feminine are used to represent the different faces of the underlying force fundamental to the continuation of life and of our universe (Gafini, 2003). The Bible also portrays the 'Mercy Seat' at the top of the Ark of the Covenant as involving two cherubs, facing each other with their wings extended, but does not make reference to their sexual embrace (Romer, 1988). This lack of embrace highlights the Christian departure from Hebrew tradition in relation to sexuality.

As captured in the cherub embrace, or in the Hebrew mysticism of eros, Judaism regards sex as a 'divine gift' from God, not solely for the purpose of procreation, but critically for companionship and pleasure. In effect, sex is the cord that secures the union of two lovers for life, facilitating shared strength, pleasure and ease, as well as for the rearing of children (Wouk, 1959). The term sex, meaning the interaction between husband and wife, comes from *Yod-Dalet-Ayin*, meaning, 'to know', thus illustrating that sexuality involves the heart and mind and not merely the body. Judaism acknowledges sexuality as a strong and chronic urge, similar to hunger or thirst, that is apparent in healthy human beings. However, whilst Judaism regards sex as a healthy and necessary part of a couple's life, it also asserts that the purpose of the sexual relationship within the bounds of a marriage, is primarily to satisfy the needs of the woman. Thus, if a man, for whatever reason, cannot 'satisfy' his wife, he should, respectfully, offer divorce so that she can seek fulfilment with another.

The same is not true for Christianity, which some describe as 2nd generation Judaism. In Christianity, marriage is a spiritual matter, between man and wife, for according to the Bible, man and wife are one. Christianity also suggests that it is better to remain unmarried, namely, as Jesus. However, if individuals cannot control themselves, it is better that they marry than burn with lust! Thus, sex in marriage is for procreation, not pleasure.

From the European perspective, the French historian Michel Foucault (1979), in drawing upon ancient Greek and Christian teaching, argues, as Plato did, that the control of the body was fundamental for appropriate conduct of social and political life. However, the simpler European past drew few distinctions between public and private life. In fact, open displays of sexual behaviour were quite common (Keegan, 1988). That was to change in the middle ages. Cleugh (1963) illustrates through Bede's (672–735) writings, that in medieval monasteries, convents and churches, outrageous sexual behaviour presented a major problem. Manuscripts from the seventh and eighth centuries reveal that punishment for different classes of sexual misconduct were calculated in elaborate detail (Cleugh, 1963). Some of the most extreme offences called for castration, while others required extensive penance (Cleugh, 1963). A monk found guilty of simple fornication with unmarried persons could expect to fast for a year on bread and water, while a nun could expect three to seven years of fasting and a bishop 12 years (Cleugh, 1963). The very fact that these schedules existed indicates the extent to which these behaviours posed a challenge to the order and routine of these early forms of organisation (Cleugh, 1963; Burrell, 1984; Morgan, 1986).

Scrutiny of workplace sexuality continued into the industrial revolution. For example, the British *Factory Act of 1833* gave attention to controlling sexual behaviour at work, whereby, the industrial masters espoused the virtues of abstinence, restraint and clean living (Morgan, 1986). Through the pursuit of such values, certain historians promote the case that repressed sexuality shapes the nature of an organisation (Morgan, 1986). On this basis it has been argued that employees identify work as an outlet for repressed sexuality. Morgan (1986) pursues a Freudian argument that acquiring control over the body hinges on social pressures. Thus, the discipline to appropriately respond gives rise to the dominance of the anal personality, namely someone highly controlling who needs structure and routines (Freud, 1927). In effect, social controls institutionalise a redirection of sexual energy, repressing gentile sexuality whilst allowing and encouraging the expression of anal eroticism in subliminal form. This line of thought emphasises that repressed anal sexuality considerably underlies the development of industrial society.

With the onset of the *Information Age*, and the emerging 'global village' where working from multiple locations is becoming reality, especially since laptops and cell-phones stretch the office all the way home, distinction between public and private life has again become increasingly blurred. Within this context, sexuality and sexual health are more freely talked about and researched. For example, the 1994 United Nations' (UN) committee's draft-plan for the International Conference on Population and Development held in Cairo, defines 'sexual health' as 'the integration of the romantic, emotional, intellectual and social aspects of sexual being' (Elliott and Dickey, 1994). The document also suggests that 'governments should use television soap operas and other traditional media to encourage discussion of sensitive topics' (Elliott and Dickey, 1994: 58). Through so doing, parallels can be drawn between the diverse nature of the home/work interface and pre medieval society's merging of the private/public interface.

The greater 'laxity' of the information age seems equally to have influenced the western church. Clerical celibacy, long held a sacred value in the Catholic tradition, has increasingly been questioned by the laity and some members of the clergy alike. The issue of clergy intimacy and sexual behaviour has been raised by several high-profile cases of sexually active clergy who fathered children while continuing publicly to uphold church teaching. One example is of the former Irish Bishop of Galway, Dr Eamon Casey, who 'fled in disgrace' to South Africa after a woman named Annie Murphy wrote the book, *Forbidden Fruit*, based on their affair which led to the birth of their son Peter (*Irish Examiner*, 2000; de Rossa and Murphy, 1993). Further, the high-profile Irish 'showbiz' priest, the late Fr Michael Cleary, was equally discovered to have fathered a child. Ironically, both men played a key part in the Pope's 1979 visit to Galway, and both have since been exposed as causing 'needless scandal' within the Catholic Church (*Irish Examiner*, 2000).

Similarly, a former British Bishop, made a public statement that he planned to marry the woman he had first encountered while counselling her during her divorce (CWN, 2003). The Bishop caused scandal not only for his abrupt disappearance and the subsequent revelation of his relationship with the woman in question, but also by his admission that he had fathered a child with another woman 15 years before and also by selling his story to British tabloids (CWN, 2003).

Another story to recently capture the headlines is that of the first Church of England openly gay nomination of Canon Jeffrey John for the position of Bishop of Reading, UK, in 2003. Although Dr John declared his celibacy, he failed to gain approval and withdrew his candidacy (BBC News, 2003). In the same year, the first publicly acknowledged ordination of a gay clergyman as Bishop of the Episcopal Church, V. Gene Robinson, as Bishop of New Hampshire, has led to dissension in the Church, the reverberations of which have not yet fed through the system (Associated Press, 2003).

In response to growing concern and unwelcome publicity, in February 2004, the General Synod of the Church of England gave its final approval to a proposed ten-point code guideline outlining the professional conduct of clergy, setting standards for vicars when they come into contact with their congregation (Verkaik, 2004). It is emphasised that vicars avoid inappropriate touching or gestures of affection, as inappropriate physical contact can be taken to be emotional or sexually abusive. It is also highlighted that vicars should not seek sexual advantage. Archbishops, bishops, priests, vicars and deacons accused of sexual misconduct and/or bullying will be tried in private by the Church of England's new tribunals stretching across the 43 dioceses. The Clergy Disciplinary Measure (2003) sets out who will sit on the new tribunals and how complaints will be investigated. The new tribunals will replace the 900-year-old system of ecclesiastical Consistory Courts, which hear misconduct complaints. Under the new code parishioners can complain about vicars over issues of sexual misconduct and over being abusive or lazy (Verkaik, 2004). It is intended that the tribunal begin trying cases of sexual misconduct and bullying in 2005. Charges of expressing inappropriate political opinions, or pursuing doctrinal ritual or ceremonial acts which offend, remain the subject of consideration within the existing system.

In contrast, Islam's view of sexuality resembles, to a certain extent, that of Judaism. Islamic spiritual medicine (*Unani Medicine*, or *Tibb al-Nabawi*) regards celibacy as potentially dangerous, both spiritually and physically (Al-Ghazili, 1978). Sexuality is considered sacred in Islam, from both the legalistic perspective, as well as from an esoteric understanding held by Islamic mystics such as Sufis. In Islam, the world rests on the strict separation of the two 'orders', the feminine and the masculine. The unity of the world can be achieved only through harmony between man and woman, realised with their full knowledge and within the bounds of marriage (Bouhdiba, 1974). Where men hold a *ghayii* (sexual lust) and are bearers of rationality, women have *sabr* (patience, endurance, tolerance) and are bearers of emotionality (Lavie, 1990). In order to fully realise the harmony intended by God, the man should assume his masculinity and a woman her full femininity. As in Judaism, the Islamic view of the world removes guilt from the sexes and does so in order to make them available to one another and to realise a 'dialogue of the sexes' in a context of mutual respect and the *joie de vivre* of marriage (Bouhdiba, 1974).

In Hindu religion, a spectrum of approaches on how human sexuality should be addressed exists, largely dependent on how speedily one wishes to achieve *liberation* or *moksha*. At one end of the spectrum are strict disciplines, for example, as practised by Hare Krishna where, even for a married couple, sex is only permitted once a month and even then when pregnancy is desired (Radhakrishnan, 1957). As soon as the woman becomes pregnant, sexual engagement should cease. At the other end of the spectrum, are the *bhagwan rajneesh (osho)* groups, which even encourage group sex on the basis that one will 'tire' of such indulgence and eventually become more 'spiritual' and 'detached' from worldly sensual experiences (Radhakrishnan, 1957).

In Buddhism, no moral absolutes exist as diverse paths are available for people with differing needs and capacities. In Buddhism, sexuality is not based on constructs such as marriage, as marriage is a civil and not a spiritual matter. What is important is that sexuality is consensual. Thus, in Buddhism, sexual desire is unique and not harmful or perverted. The dialectics inherent in Mahvyvna Buddhism, in particular in the Tantric and Chan/Zen traditions, allow for greater laxity than that of Christianity (Faure, 1998).

Intimacy at work

As can be seen, the exhibition of libidinal energy has been evident from ancient times and in the manner in which various religions encourage or repress such drives. Sexuality is alluded to in dress and self-presentation, in jokes and gossip, in looks and flirtations, in the manner in which dalliances are pursued, in the expression of fantasy and in a range of sexually coercive behaviours (Pringle, 1996). Some even consider the expression of sexuality as the glue to every working relationship (Jones, 1972). Equally, the topic of libido is regarded by many as a sensitive, delicate, ubiquitous, taboo issue, that is poorly appreciated until wrong doing occurs as in the case of sexual harassment (Jones, 1972; Hearn and Parkin, 1987; Gutek, 1996). Irrespective of its delicacy, sexuality is an influential, underlying theme cutting across a range of discourses and interactions (Pringle, 1996).

Despite a growing interest in the area, libidinal energy manages to remain subliminal and avoid the scrutiny of empirical research. One attributable reason is that the topic violates the norms that define the rational realm of western organisation theory, leading to an arbitrary separation of 'human sexuality' and 'workplace' (Hearn and Parkin, 1987). In fact, research into intimacy was considered taboo until the mid-1970s, and as a result, aspects of this vital part of the human psyche remain poorly understood.

However, upon entering the 'rational' organisation, humans do not become asexual during the working hours. As Marcuse (1968: 12) points out, 'without ceasing to be an instrument of labour, the body is allowed to exhibit its sexual features in the everyday work world and in work relations'. Yet this more liberal view has not prevailed.

The reason is the age-old perennial tension between reason (rationality) and emotion. Early laws and codes of conduct exemplified by the Code of Hammurabi, the Ten Commandments and the Edicts of emperor Ashika are historical examples of various attempts of harnessing emotional life within the bounds of rationality. The sixteenth century humanist philosopher, Erasmus of Rotterdam, addressed the emotional/rational dichotomy (popular heart/head dilemma) in his satirical writing and offered the ratio between passion and reason bestowed on man calculated as 24:1, where anger and lust are two tyrants in opposition to reason (Erasmus, 1971: 87). On this basis, current and historical thinking has pursued the view that human passion too often overwhelms reason (Ekman, 1992: 189).

To a certain degree, there is evidence that supports this line of thought. The basic human architecture and biological design of the neural circuitry of emotion – the development of the 'limbic' (Latin, *limbus* – 'ring') system (that part of the brain that encircles the top of the brain stem) predates the development of rational thought – the 'neocortex' or the thinking brain (the grey complicated tissue that makes up the top layers of the brain). The neocortex contains the centres that plans, comprehends, perceives and co-ordinates movement. The 'emotional brain' that also aids learning and memory, developed considerably before the rational brain, where the most ancient root of emotional life is the sense of smell, 'olfactory lobe' (Goleman, 1996). Further research, in particular in neurology and psychiatry during the last century, showed that very little of the 'rhinencephalon' (the nose brain) serves olfactory functions in humans and that the greater part of the limbic system is concerned with the regulation of the affective life in the individual (Slater and Roth, 1970). Limbic structures, through control of the endocrine system generate feelings of pleasure and sexual desire, as the prime emotions that feed sexual passion (Goleman, 1996: 11). The development of the neocortex and its connection to the limbic systems further facilitates the development of the bond between partners and children, the base for the family unit and the long term commitment of childrearing. In contrast, the neocortex, as the seat of thought, gives an intellectual edge to the individual. The neocortex's myriad of interconnectivity circuits to the limbic system, gives the emotional centres immense scope and latitude to influence the functioning of rational thoughts. Thus, whilst the rational mind provides logical connections between cause and effect, the emotional mind is indiscriminate (Epstein, 1994).

Freud (1927) argued that much of emotional life is unconscious. The generative dance between the rational and emotional mind is delicate and unique to each individual, often mediated by individual experience and cultural context. Thus, the historical pre-occupation with the daily conduct of one's life requires temperance, balance and wisdom, not for the purpose of the suppression of emotions but for the expression of 'appropriate' emotions, that is feelings proportionate to the circumstances required for organised life. On this basis, one can see why the degree to which contemporary organisations and ways of working are adequately equipped to deal with appropriate expressions of intimacy in the workplace tends to be contextually (re)defined.

In fact, the emergent perspective adopted by certain feminist writers concentrates on the coercive aspects of sexuality, namely that of sexual harassment (MacKinnon, 1979). Along the same lines, Segal (1987) argues that sexual domination is based on social and economic power. In an era of increasing female empowerment and gender equity, libidinal energy is beginning to be analysed from the angles of control, influence and power. One particular aspect of control and influence pertinent in today's society is that of marketing and the drive to spend more in order to increase personal consumption. Increasing consumerism is facilitated both by communication technology and by sexuality through sexual imagery particularly that of women and less so of men (Wernick, 1987), for the purposes of selling ever more products and services.

Thus, in order to further appreciate the topic of workplace intimacy, of which sexuality is only a part, attention is given in this review of the literature to the ethics of adult sexual behaviour at work, or what some term as libidinal politics. Like Rubin (1984), who replaces the notion of a single universal ideal of sexuality with pluralistic sexual ethics, discussion concerning what is acceptable libidinal behaviour in the organisation and the impact such behaviour has on the organisation, is pursued. Within such analysis, the meaning and application of intimacy in the workplace is also examined.

'Appropriate' workplace behaviour

Aside from other purposes, workplaces are recognised as social focal points (Kakabadse and Kakabadse, 1999). Many social relationships begin at work, which involve the experience of psychological intimacy, sexual attraction between people, sexual innuendoes, the realisation of sexual desire and sexual harassment (Croteau, 1996). This has particularly been the case in the Western world over the last 50 years, as work has not only become a focal point of people's lives but also a source of ever greater wealth and spending capacity (Day and Schoenrade, 1997). With ever increasing education and affluence comes an independence of mind that, in turn, erodes the more traditional distinctions concerning work related behaviour, which means that attention increasingly focuses on the nature of appropriate behaviour for the workplace (Kakabadse and Kakabadse, 2004). It is recognised that although female representation as a percentage of the total number of directors makes gloomy reading, three per cent of executive directors in Great Britain (Singh and Vinnicombe, 2003), 4.4 per cent in New Zealand (Pajo *et al*, 1997) and about five per cent in Canada (Burrke, 1994), women are increasingly entering the formerly male-dominated domains and assuming positions which involve frequent interaction with men (Johnston, 1997). Further, women's entry into the professional/technical occupations is also slowly increasing, although the low starting point needs to be recognised. Professional/technical occupations, defined as 'persons employed in technical work for which the normal qualification is a degree in science, maths or engineering' (McRea *et al*, 1991: 7), attracted one per cent of UK women in 1979, but rose to seven per cent in 1994 (Glover *et al*, 1996). The feminist movement of recent decades, the mass entrance of women into the work force, the increasing number of female managers (Powell *et al*, 1984) and the increasing number of promotions of women to leadership positions, have shifted societal gender-role perceptions (Helmrich *et al*, 1982). In so doing, the formerly more clear, unambiguous roles and status of the sexes has become blurred (Ibarra, 1993). In the industrialised past, close work relationship consisted of 'psychological intimacy', often between members of the same sex, ranging from assembly line, to boardroom, to typing pool, to nursing unit relations. Currently, increasingly close working relationships are being built between co-workers of the same and opposite sex. Close interactions between the sexes are forged by the sheer nature of task related work and equally by the organisation through emphasising team building and networking.

The socio-economic shift to a diversified labour force has attracted recent interest in intimacy based research of which sex comparison (biological based categories of difference between males and females) and gender belief systems (psychological features frequently associated with these biological sets, assigned either by an observer or by the individual subject), occupy prominent places (Ely, 1995; Kent and Moss, 1994). One perspective adopted in pursuing a study of explicit and implicit sex and gender-roles differences, and differences of attitude between males and females, has been to assume a stability between these differences, stripped of the context from which they arose (Misheler, 1979). For example, Gilligan's (1982) work on the sex-differentiated patterns of moral development, suggests a broad range of disposition of differences between the sexes. Others identify differences in latent or exhibited aggression between the sexes (Maccoby and Jacklin, 1974; 1980), whilst others challenge the possible causes of such differences (Tieger, 1980).

The alternative view is that behaviourally based differences ebb and flow with changes and circumstance and that stereotypes are an unstable unit of analysis to examine as they vary according to time and organisational and ethnic culture (Deaux, 1985: 69). Fradrich and Ferrell's (1992) research supports this view, as their study suggests that 85 per cent of their respondents changed their moral philosophy perspective between work and non-work situations according to the context in which they find themselves. Similarly, Lifton (1984) finds no gender differences in terms of level of moral reasoning.

It is also suggested that the concepts of masculinity and femininity are not precise correlations of biological sex (Bem, 1974). Certain researchers suggest that with female advancement into leadership positions, women today possess more masculine characteristics than they have at any time in the past (Kent and Moss, 1994). Branner *et al* (1989), for example, concludes that females in non-traditional professions, such as management, have rejected gender stereotypes. Similarly, Powell and Butterfield (1979), find that female students on Master's of Business Administration (MBA) degree courses rate themselves higher on masculinity than femininity.

Emerging out of the growing awareness of sexuality in society and particularly in the workplace, sexual harassment and censure of sexual activity hold a critical preoccupation. The violation of the individual and the public relations damage that sexual harassment law suits can have on the organisation, seems to have unwittingly influenced the thinking behind the actions to be taken if two heterosexual colleagues are discovered '*in flagrante delicto*' in the office (Hall, 1996). In effect, the closer interaction of the sexes in the workplace has encouraged the re-emergence of the medieval preoccupation, namely, sexually based moral judgement.

Yet, considerable disagreement exists as to what constitutes moral judgement, due to the fact that people adopt varying personal ethics (Sharp, 1989). On the one hand, certain researchers have analysed the relationship between cognitive style based on Jungian personality types and business ethics (Fleming, 1985; McIntyre and Capen, 1993). Others adopt a moral philosophy platform driven by the accepted dominant religions, Christianity, Buddhism, Hinduism, Islam, Judaism (Cavanagh *et al*, 1981; Arthur, 1984). In particular, Judo-Christian ethical frameworks stem from two broad categories, teleological and deontological. Teleological based philosophy addresses moral worth from the view of the consequences of human behaviour. In contrast to the greatest good for the greatest number ethic, deontology focuses on the intentions and methods of human behaviour but not on ends. The moral right of a course of action, irrespective of its consequences, forms the basis of deontological reasoning. Bluntly put, the teleological interpretation of sexual occurrences in the workplace would be, 'Just what would others think and say?', whereas the more traditional deontological perspective would be, 'Sexual activity at work is simply wrong no matter who it is and why it occurred!'.

However, irrespective of the conceptual platforms for ethical understanding and 'moral' decision making, observers identify that the lengths to which an individual proceeds is influenced by both the moral rightness of the issue confronting them and their surrounding circumstances (Jones, 1991). Thus, with the re-awakening of medieval Cartesian thinking, teleological sentiments considerably influence how workplace sexual behaviour is judged and nowhere more so than in differentiating intimacy from harassment (Pierce, 1997).

Harassment

The terms intimacy, sexuality and harassment have been adopted interchangeably. Whilst romantic relationships at work or 'office romances' (sexual and non-sexual) are characterised by jointly or mutually desired interaction between two members of the same organisation, the unwelcome sexual attention directed towards an employee of the organisation is considered as harassment (Pierce *et al*, 1996; Pierce and Aguinis, 2001). The European Commission (EC) defines sexual harassment as 'unwanted conduct of a sexual nature, or conduct based on sex, affecting the dignity of women and men at work' (Rubenstein, 1988: 4). Although, in most cases a clear difference exists between intimate/romantic behaviour in the workplace and sexual harassment, what constitutes such behaviour is open to interpretation. Harassment in the workplace can take a variety of forms, such as physical conduct, jokes, offensive language, gossip, slander, sectarian songs, letters, posters, graffiti, obscene gestures, flags, bunting and emblems, isolation or non-cooperation and exclusion from social activities, coercion for sexual favours, pressure to participate in political/religious groups, and intrusion by pestering, spying and stalking (IPD, 1997). Sexual harassment has to have a sexual intent or be perceived by the receiver as having sexual intent. Therefore, 'it is for each individual to determine what behaviour is acceptable to them, and what they regard as offensive' (European Commission, 1991: 16). Moreover, intimate/ romantic relations and sexual harassment also share two common elements, they both entail some form of sexual interaction between two employees and are related to the workplace. Thus, sexual harassment or behaviour that is unwelcome, unwanted and unreciprocated is a subjective concept, namely, philosophically teleological in nature and relies as much, if not more, upon the impact of that behaviour on the recipient, as opposed to the intent of the instigator (Kiely and Henbest, 2000). Further, the EC distinguishes between sexual harassment which damages the employee's working environment, and sexual harassment used as the basis for employment decisions affecting the harassed victim's, promotion, appraisal and overall future (European Commission, 1991).

Further, adopting a societal and organisational power perspective provides additional explanation regarding sexual harassment (Apodaca and Kleiner, 2001; Sprecher, 1985). Theories based on societal/ historical power view relationships as behaviour emergent from historical/cultural attitudes and beliefs related to sex roles, where sexual harassment is perceived as a consequence of cultural influence and culturally legitimated power and status differences, rather than being unique to the workplace (Malovich and Stake, 1990; Barak *et al*, 1995). On this basis, sexual harassment results from power and status inequality within the organisation (Gruber, 1992). Although, sexual harassment is perceived as an abuse of power in order to sexually coerce or intimidate another, other factors also facilitate power projection, such as opportunity, gender ratios and implicitly understood organisational norms (Stringer *et al*, 1990; Crain and Heischmidt, 1995). For example, certain studies have shown that inappropriate gender-based expectations can arise when an organisation is predominated by one gender (Gutek, 1985). The predominant group unduly influences the expectations and the treatment of the other gender (Fitzgerald and Shullman, 1993). A sexual harassment study based on a 20,000 survey response of military personnel world-wide, through the UK's Defence Manpower Data Centre, reports that 64 per cent of females and 17 per cent of males have been sexually harassed (Webb, 1991). Although, research shows that women have experienced greater harassment than men, partly as a result of entering into traditionally male-dominated professions (Rosell *et al*, 1995), emerging evidence also indicates that sexual harassment of men is on the rise (Townsend and Luthar, 1995).

Ever greater numbers of sexual harassment incidences are being reported in the USA. In 1991 the Equal Employment Opportunity Commission (EEOC) dealt with 6,212 cases whilst in 1997, 15,889 cases were recorded (*The Economist,* 1998b). Further, certain studies claim that between 25 per cent and 50 per cent of women in the US labour force have experienced unwanted sexual attention and gender based harassment (Apodaca and Kleiner, 2001; Gelfand *et al,* 1995).

In the US, sexual harassment is considered to be an act that can take the form of speech and/or sex-biased behaviour, is sexually discriminating, is deliberate, is neither welcomed nor encouraged, and involves an abuse of power, committed by, or permitted by, superiors (Apodaca and Kleiner, 2001). The US Merit System Protection board lists the seven most frequent forms of harassment in order of frequency (Smalensky and Kleiner, 2001: 4):

- teasing, jokes, remarks or questions of a sexual nature,
- pressuring for dates,
- letters, telephone calls, or materials of a sexual nature,
- sexual looks or gestures,
- deliberate touching, leaning over or cornering,
- pressure in order to be granted sexual favours,
- actual or attempted rape or sexual assault.

Although initial US sexual harassment polices were oriented towards women they were updated in the early 1990s to include homosexual harassment as well (Baker *et al*, 1990). Under US law, sexual harassment is considered as two kinds, *quid pro quo*, ('this for that') and that of interacting (working) in a sexually hostile environment (Silvam and Kleiner, 2001). The first relates to hierarchical structure and power-relationships and the latter refers to unlawful gender discrimination (Silvam and Kleiner, 2001).

Noteworthy is that issues of bullying and harassment are often discussed interchangeably. Analysis of various definitions emphasises that bullying is an abuse of power, although not necessarily with the superior as aggressor (Field, 1997; MSF, 1994; 1995; Adams, 1992). Bullying may involve verbal intimidation that would most likely occur in the presence of colleagues, undermining of the victims' professional work and with the perpetrator taking credit for other people's work. Bullying may also involve physical violence (MSF, 1994; Field, 1997) and extremes of ostracism. Unnecessary high levels of supervision are also characteristic signs of bullying behaviour (MSF, 1994; Field, 1997). At times, the characteristics of bullying may not be recognised and passed off as personality based conflict. Harassment, on the other hand, is orientated towards a particular characteristic of the victim, thus leading to various forms of harassment, such as sexual based according to gender, or sexual preference, racial based according to ethnic background and sectarian based in according to religion (Collier, 1995).

Intimacy

The contrast to the moral judgement position of what is right and wrong behaviour, including that of bullying and harassment, is that intimacy is a natural occurrence in the workplace. In effect, the pre-medieval view of 'that's the way life is', and boundaries such as those between work and home are unnatural, becomes the alternative perspective. As more people increasingly spend more time within the workplace, close friendships between men and women at work are becoming an increasingly common experience. Friendship is viewed as a voluntary, reciprocal, equal relationship which is seen as possibly unique and probably special, and which enhances the sense of self of each of the partners (Wright, 1985). Friendships between same-sex and opposite-sex colleagues takes many forms such as (Rubin, 1970; Sternberg, 1986; Pierce *et al*, 1996):

- an exchange of personal disclosures,
- affection and respect,

- passionate desire to be in the presence of one's friend or romantic partner,
- pleasant emotional state such as need satisfaction, happiness and sexual gratification,
- psychological arousal and the desire for a sexual act with one's partner.

Distinction is made between intimacy based on personal attraction or 'liking', and intimacy based on romantic attraction or 'loving', with the former being recognised as a prelude for more intense, romantic and loving feelings (Sternberg, 1986). Work colleagues may develop relationships that are intimate in a myriad of ways, which only ultimately may emerge as sexual intimacy. From the historical and religious analysis already undertaken, such an emerging perspective from the literature is nothing new, as individuals seek to find, establish or experience multilevel interpersonal connections at work. Sexual intimacy may grow out of one or more of these connections, or may stay as liking or 'platonic'. Sternberg (1986) distinguishes between 'liking' and 'loving' feelings in relationships and proposes a triangular theory of love that holds that all loving relationships are based on three components (Fig. 2.1):

- Intimacy – close, connected, bonding feelings in a relationship,
- Passion – drivers that foster romance, physical attraction, and sexual consummation,
- Decision/commitment – decision that one is in love with someone and ultimately a commitment to continue loving that person.

Expressing love in a relationship requires actions illustrative of these three components, such as (Sternberg, 1986: 132),

- Intimacy:
    - Communicating inner feelings,
    - Promoting others' well-being,
    - Expressing empathy for the other, and,
    - Offering emotional and material support to the other.
- Passion:
    - Kissing
    - Hugging
    - Gazing
    - Touching
    - Petting
    - Making love

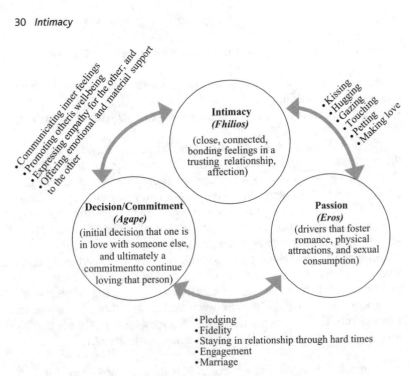

Figure 2.1 Loving Relationships
Source: Compiled and adapted from Sternberg (1986)

- Decision/commitment:
  - Pledging
  - Fidelity
  - Remaining in relationship through hard times
  - Engagement
  - Marriage

Building on the work of Rubin (1970), Sternberg (1986) and Lobel *et al* (1994), other scholars (Pierce *et al*, 1996; Powell and Foley, 1998) have argued that the three components of intimacy, passion and decision/ commitment, produce a variety of different relationships depending on each component(s) absence or presence and that only 'complete' love consists of all three components. From such analysis six types of relationships are identified (Pierce *et al*, 1996: 7; Powell and Foley, 1998: 431):

- liking, involves only intimacy without any intense feelings of passion or commitment,

- infatuated love, involves immediate and passionate physiological arousal without feelings of intimacy or commitment,
- romantic love, encompasses both intimacy and passion with arousal instigated by physical attraction and a strong emotional bond,
- fatuous love, feelings of arousal or passion, but an absence of intimacy and feelings of bondedness,
- consummate love, a 'complete' love that encompasses the intimacy, passion and decision/commitment components, and
- non-loving, lacking intimacy, passion and commitment.

Despite the contribution of Sternberg (1986) and his colleagues, from a scientific perspective, love is an elusive concept as the range of psychological, social and cultural meanings it attracts are limitless (Borgatta and Borgatta, 1992). Various typologies of attributes, emotions and behaviour have been identified intermingled with varying styles of living and, in turn, loving (Lasswell and Lasswell, 1980; Sternberg, 1986; Kemper, 1988; Borgatta and Borgatta, 1992). Additionally, the concept of love varies from one culture to another and from one historical era to another (Murstein, 1974; Hunt, 1959). Thus, additional to the characteristics of the individuals involved or of their relationship, people's experience of love is influenced by the context in which their sentiments are formed. For some, the initial experience of love begins with physical symptoms, palpitations, rapid breathing, sweating and other symptoms that are essentially similar to those associated with emotions such as fear, although it is acknowledged that such outcomes are also context and culture specific (Borgatta and Borgatta, 1992). Others pursue sexual encounters in the absence of any romantic feelings, possibly derived from a human biological heritage, or more likely through learned cultural patterns (Borgatta and Borgatta, 1992). Hence, romantic relationships, often encompassing sexually motivated behaviour attracts a cluster of cultural expectations (Merrill, 1959), highlighting certain gender differences with respect to love and living as much arising from culturally defined sex roles and social expectations (Borgatta and Borgatta, 1992). However, in whichever country or culture, workplace intimacy does engender a response, which, at times, can emerge as extreme reactions.

With that in mind, the question arises as to why people become intimately 'inter-tangled'? A variety of reasons is identified.

- Love motive, 'consummate relationship' desire for intimacy, passion and decision/commitment (Quinn, 1977; Sternberg, 1986).

- Job motive, desire for advancement, job security, financial reward (Quinn, 1977; Mainiero, 1986).
- Ego motive, desire for excitement, adventure, personal satisfaction reward (Quinn, 1977).
- Power motive, desire to increase self importance/influence (Mainiero, 1986).
- Utilitarian motive, ego for one and job motive for other, alternatively job for both (Quinn, 1977).
- Dependency motive, desire for support and 'protection' (Mainiero, 1986).
- Proximity motive, need to be liked, attractive to others or a special other (Byrne and Neuman, 1992; Pierce *et al*, 1996).

In further analysing the dependency motive, Mainiero (1986) identifies three types of dependencies influencing workplace relationships:

- Task dependency, where an employee depends on others to perform their function effectively.
- Career dependency, whereby the individual who desires advancement in the organisation depends on the consent of the other for advancement, typified by a hierarchical relationship.
- Personal/sexual dependency, often exhibited in hierarchical relationships that can undermine both task and career dependency.

However, the components of intimacy are dynamic and evolve over time. Sternberg (1986) argues that intimacy, passion and the decision/commitment required to sustain loving relationships seldom remain constant. Bearing in mind the dynamism, particularly of working life, the question remains concerning the initiating motivators of intimate relationships and the ensuing consequences of such emotions.

A particular motivator is proximity, which in turn, presents opportunity and induces exposure, and thus, can elicit an affective response such as liking (Byrne and Neuman, 1992; Pierce *et al*, 1996). Proximity offers people the opportunity to work near one another, interact frequently and obtain information concerning the people with whom they work and wish to become more intimate (Anderson and Hunsaker, 1985). Both physical proximity (actual physical distance between two individuals) and functional proximity (ease of dyadic instruction) promote the occurrence of intimacy (Pierce *et al*, 1996). Research supports the initial findings of Segal (1987: 654) that the 'smaller the physical and functional distance between two people, the more likely they are to be attracted to each other'. For example, Schor (1991) established that attraction increases in both task-oriented and work-related settings. Such attraction is further prompted when employees are required to spend long hours together, which in turn leads to greater frequency of social interaction between people who are similarly work engaged, thereby increasing the likelihood of inter-personal attraction (Mainiero, 1989; Byrne and Neuman, 1992).

Additionally, on-going workplace development activities, such as training programmes, exposure to mentoring, and supervision, and business trips are identified as key drivers to facilitating work related intimacy (Quinn, 1977; Lobel *et al*, 1994). The current vogue for focusing on group work and working towards the same goal, promotes within employees the feeling of a 'unit', a view that can prompt positive feelings towards team colleagues (Anderson and Hunsaker, 1985). In order to be even more competitive, strategies that encourage team-building, networking and coalition building, intensify employee interaction and the need for employees to gain collegial social support, which in turn strengthens work-related relationships (Lobel *et al*, 1994). Collegial social support may involve (Lobel *et al*, 1994: 10):

- Emotional support, nurturing, providing empathy, caring, trusting, listening to problems, prompting the other's happiness.
- Instrumental support, providing assistance for colleagues in need, such as doing aspects of their work for them.
- Informational support, providing counselling, advice, or other information that helps the individual cope.
- Appraisal support, which involves coaching and or feedback about performance which individuals use to evaluate themselves.

For example, the mentoring, coaching and team building training and development exercises promote 'we-ness', the bonding of group partners to share the belief that they are motivated by considerations of the other's welfare, not merely for their own self-satisfaction but for that of the work unit (Bowes-Sperry and Tata, 1999). Under such circumstances, intimate relationships are naturally engendered as individuals grow accustomed to positive emotional responses and become more secure in a relationship experienced as selfless rather than selfish (Waring *et al*, 1980: 26). Such sentiments are identified as particularly evident in service organisations, where emotionally driven interaction predominates over economic rationality (Arnould and Price, 1993).

Engendering 'extraordinary' service experiences, such as river rafting trips, which are 'inherently interpretative and affective' promotes the notion of emotional inputs and outcomes, rather than encourage transactionality (Arnould and Price, 1993: 28). Similar dynamics can work in cross-gender mentoring relationships, where the potential for sexual involvement between mentor and protégé increases due to the intensity of the mentoring relationship (Clawson and Kram, 1984; Ragins, 1989; Fitt and Newton, 1981; Collins, 1983a; Powell *et al*, 1984).

Technological advances that allow for a 7 day working week and a management drive to increasingly facilitate gains in productivity, results in many people working harder and longer than before. For example, recent research indicates that Americans are working 160 hours more per year than was the case 25 years ago (Gibbs, 1998; Chomsky, 2000). Similarly, according to a survey by the Department of Trade and Industry (DTI), Britons have the longest working week in Europe, an average of 43.6 hours a week, compared to the European average of 40.3 hours (DTI, 2002). The same study also highlights that one in six employees are working more than 60 hours a week, compared to one in eight, two years ago. Those who work 60 hours or more are principally young people, as 21 per cent of 30 to 39-year-olds work 60 hours or more compared to just 14 per cent of the over-40s (DTI, 2002). A similar study conducted on behalf of *The Observer* newspaper by ICM Research (*The Observer*, 2003), identified similar trends concerning longer working hours, particularly comparing Britain against that of continental Europe. Additionally, the ICM survey discovered that 57 per cent of women state they are now working longer hours against 48 per cent of men (*The Observer*, 2003). Such difference is attributed to the fact that women are 'catching up' with their male counterparts in terms of pay but also of working conditions. The same ICM sample was asked whether they would sleep more, or have sex, given an extra hour in bed. Thirty eight per cent of men chose sleep in comparison to 67 per cent of women who would opt for sleep (*The Observer*, 2003). Aside from needing to sleep longer, a further study claims that the current environment in the workplace is having a negative impact on the basis of managerial performance (HR Gateway 2003). Based on a recent survey, it is concluded that,

- 54 per cent of managers feel inadequate when it comes to driving team performance and similarly for,
- 53 per cent in influencing staff,

- 52 per cent in motivating staff,
- 51 per cent in coaching.

The study goes on to suggest that just over 50 per cent of managers feel themselves as wanting in the area of building relationships and thus are more vulnerable to handling 'emotionally charged' circumstances. The report highlights a number of training and development initiatives that organisations should urgently introduce.

As 73 per cent of UK private and public sector managers claim that their workload has increased, people are more obliged to find fulfilment, friendships and affirmation in their jobs (Bunting, 2001). People have less discretionary time to maintain private relationships and so search for special support in the workplace. Therefore, the emerging, urgent debate is not about recognising how much we invest in our jobs, but about how little we invest in our lives outside the office (Bunting, 2001).

Concern over the impact of work on family life in the UK prompted a further DTI enquiry on how to provide for greater balance between work and home through greater support for parents (DTI, 2003). The report concludes that,

- Government intervention to help parents 'balance' work and family responsibilities is important (DTI, 2003: 1),
- revision of the tax and benefits systems are required particularly through the creation of the Child's Tax Credit and the Working Tax Credit, providing for more cash in the wage packet of lower income earners,
- greater care for children's needs should be paid for through increases in maternity pay, extension of the duration of maternity pay (from 18 to 26 weeks) and the introduction of rights for parents of young, disabled children to request a more flexible working day,
- greater funding is required for child care and, at present, additional funding for the development of Child Care Centres has been committed so that 250,000 new child care places will be created,
- flexible working is now a key national issue as dual earner and lone parent families have dramatically increased,
- the private sector should work far more in partnership with parents to promote flexible working.

In fact, the Trades Union Congress (TUC), in effect, the 'Corporate Centre' of trade unions in the UK, has declared a campaign against the long work hours culture (TUC, Working Life, 2003). The reasons for the campaign are,

- four million people in the UK work longer than 48 hours per week (700,000 more than in 1992 when long hours protection did not exist),
- only one in three knows that a law exist protecting them from working more than 48 hours,
- two out of three who work more than 48 hours per week, according to the TUC, have been approached to opt out of working time regulations,
- one in four admit to being given no choice when signing an opt out giving away their rights,
- three out of five wish to work fewer hours and four out of five mothers wish their partners to work the normal 48 hour week because of the damage being inflicted on family life,
- the rapid increase in stress related visits to doctors is directly related to people's jobs.

The anti long work hours campaign initiated by the TUC has received backing from a recently conducted survey by a market research organisation, Datamonitor (Milmo, 2003). The survey introduced a new term, 'down shifters', namely people who give up their high paid jobs for an easier and more simplistic life style. In fact, the Datamonitor survey estimates that four million people in the UK will 'down shift' their earning capacity and wealth by 2007. The same report also states that approximately 12 million people in Europe have currently 'down shifted' their earning capacity, a figure that is expected to reach 16 million by 2007. And why? Well all of this is for less stress, a healthier life style and 'more sex' (Milmo, 2003: 3).

Additionally, certain studies show that demographic characteristics such as age, status, tenure, gender and level of education, influence the likelihood of romance in the workplace (Dillard and Witteman, 1985). Collins (1983b) argues that men in their mid-life transition are more likely to become intimately involved with a woman in the workplace. Research into generation management, especially with regard to 'generation X' and their 'baby boomer' bosses (Table 2.1) indicates that cohabitation and 'premarital' sex are common and that marriage has changed from 'commitment' or 'family values' to personal gratification realised through the ideal of romantic love (Lawes, 1999; DTS-UT, 2000). However, the counter is that the 'generation X' happiness basis of relationships is that they divorce when their expectations are

Table 2.1   Generations Values Outlook

Generation	Attributes
Silent Generation (1925–1942)	Hard working, economically conscious and trusting of government. Optimistic about the future. Hold strong set of moral obligations.
Baby Boom Generation (1943–1960)	Held strong set of ideals and traditions. Family-oriented. Fearful of the future. Politically conservative but active and socially liberal.
Generation X (1961–1980)	Live in and for the present. Like to experiment. Expect immediate results. Xers are viewed as selfish and cynical, but dependent on parents. They question authority. Feel they carry the burden of the previous generations.
Generation Y (or Echo Boom) (1981–1994)	Viewed as materialistic, selfish and disrespectful but also aware of the world. Are technologically literate. Trying to grow-up too fast. Feel they have no good role models to look towards.

Source: Compiled from DTS-UT (2000)

unfulfilled (Lawes, 1999). In the UK, currently, three quarters of all couples live together before they marry. Today, approximately, 40 per cent of births are conceived outside marriage, not quite the practice of 1800 where almost 60 per cent of all first births took place outside marriage (*The Economist*, 1998a).

Some writers argue that a more liberal outlook to workplace relations is likely to continue as 'generation Y', which is 60 million strong in the USA, is just beginning to enter the workforce. Their different attitudes and belief systems will promote different workplace dynamics due to their more materialistic nurturing that focuses on input rather than output accomplishment (Hill, 2002). However, the 'spoilt brat' dependency syndrome is already challenged as today's unpredictable work environment of mergers and acquisitions, satisfying shareholder aspirations and continuous attention to costs, lends itself to conformity, acceptance of authority and the adoption of a survival mentality (Bowman *et al*, 2002). People are too fearful to challenge for fear of loss of job and the prospect of no other, or a lesser, job to go to!

Barriers and consequences

Studies of romantic relationships reveal a broad variance of perceptions concerning the risks associated with intimate work related relationships, with certain risks being more salient for some than others (Winstead *et al*, 1995; Mainiero, 1986; 1989). Research shows that the risks of conducting intimate relations in the workplace are associated with (Mainiero, 1986; 1989),

* loss of collegiate respect,
* loss of self-image and esteem, after the discovery of an intimate relationship with another high-level colleague,
* marital strife, divorce and family disruption,
* violation of workplace norms, depending on the professional culture or code of conduct of the organisation or department. For example, Brunel University and University College London (UCL) clearly set out policy guidelines for professional conduct should sexual or romantic relationships occur in the workplace.

Other risks are associated with the fear – through being dumped, betrayed, or 'felt' to be used (Winstead *et al*, 1995).

The consequences of intimate workplace relationships are identified as partly influenced by the behaviour and attitudes of the individuals engaged in intimacy, the reaction of their colleagues and group members and the impact of the ongoing relationship on the team, department and/or the organisation as a whole (Powel and Foley, 1998). Quinn (1977) found that negative changes can occur to both participants due to their preoccupation with their relationship and thus they become less punctual, miss important meetings and commitments, make mistakes and cover-up the mistakes of their partner.

In hierarchical relationships, the consequences could include,

* ignoring complaints concerning their partners performance, should that person be in a subordinate position (Quinn, 1977),
* enhancing their partners power should they be in a subordinate role (Quinn, 1977),
* displaying favouritism towards the subordinate in terms of task assignments, pay rises and promotion (Quinn, 1977),
* negative consequences for their protégé in terms of task assignment, pay rise and promotion (Clawson and Kram, 1984),
* lower productivity for one or both partners (Pierce *et al*, 1996).

Despite the career and personal downsides associated with intimate relationships, such experiences do not prevent people from forming new relationships within the work situation. Research suggests that for those fearful of the consequences of intimacy but yet enter into a romantic relationship, their interactions are reported as more restricted and less comfortable due to their expectations of being discovered, namely, losing control of the situation (Winstead *et al*, 1995). Such individuals are also identified as making more superficial disclosures to others concerning the 'up beat' nature of their personal lives (Winstead *et al*, 1995). Further, intimate associations for men are perceived to carry more risk than for women, partly due to the common stereotype of men as unfeeling and women as loving, caring and nurturing (Winstead *et al*, 1995).

In contrast, other studies have found that workplace romances have a significant positive relationship on productivity (Pierce *et al*, 1996; Dillard, 1987; BNA,1988; Dillard and Miller, 1988; Lobel *et al*, 1994; Dillard and Broetzmann, 1989). The performance of the individual increases and their positive mindset encourages greater enthusiasm within their team. This is attributed to the fact that love-motivated individuals may attempt to,

- impress their partners,
- alleviate line manager fears that the romance will have a negative impact on work,
- devote more time and energy to job related requirements due to their greater level of commitment and personal satisfaction.

Still other studies indicate that it is impossible to predict positive or negative consequences in the workplace as the reaction of others varies from approval, tolerance, gossip and the expression of objection towards the participants and/or their managers (Quinn, 1977). Thus workplace romance consequences vary depending upon (Dillard, 1987; Dillard and Miller, 1988; Powell and Foley, 1998),

- how others perceive the nature of the intimate relationship (job-related, non-job related, illicit, non-illicit),
- management's reactions ('equity sensitivity', perceived justice, strong, weak or severe),
- the degree of disruption to the work group, department or even overall organisation,
- conflicts of interest,
- proximity to other participants (physical, functional, social),
- an assessment as to whether the effects of the romance are immediate or long-term,
- the culture and prevalent attitudes within the unit/organisation, and
- each individual's beliefs about workplace romances.

A positive collegial response is more likely when the perceived motive of the relationship is love or the fact that both of the participants are of high status (Devine and Markiewicz, 1990). Contrastingly, intimacy that is perceived to be motivated by job enhancement and hierarchical or power/exploitative reasons (especially where the woman is more senior), damaging gossip, and in some cases, complaints and ostracism may arise, which, in turn, has a negative impact on group morale (Quinn, 1977; Devine and Markiewicz, 1990; Pierce *et al*, 1996). Moreover, the prevailing culture(s) of the workplace influence not only management's response but also the dynamics, formation and consequences of workplace intimacy (Powell and Foley, 1998). A more conservatively minded organisation may induce workplace romances to go 'underground' and consequently promote collusion in keeping such 'dalliances' secret (Mainiero, 1989). In extreme cases, sexual involvement at work has engendered deep resentment and even lawsuits (Lobel *et al*, 1994).

An additional area of tension is the dissolution of the relationship. Pierce and Aguinis (2001) suggest that should a workplace romance be dissolved unilaterally, the non-initiator of the dissolution is more likely to instigate charges of sexually harassing behaviour toward his or her former romantic partner. The ending of sexually intimate power-based relationships (mentor, supervisor or subordinate) have a higher propensity to turn into accusations of sexual harassment (Powell, 1986a; Bordwin, 1994; Lobel *et al*, 1994; Mainiero, 1989), which, in turn, are more likely to have a negative influence on the careers of one or both participants (Ford and McLaughlin, 1987; Mainiero, 1989; Powell, 1986b). However, where bilaterally dissolved workplace romances occur, a much lower incidence of charges of sexual harassment are likely to arise (Pierce and Aguinis, 2001). Consequently, the pursuit and effect of workplace romance are influenced by each partner's primary motives, their social power or influence, the manner of initiation of the relationship's dissolution, the male (or female) partner's sexual harassment proclivity, the nature of each partner's residual affective state, and the organisation's tolerance for sexual harassment (Pierce and Aguinis, 2001).

The response of the organisation to intimacy in the workplace ranges from (Quinn, 1977; Pierce *et al*, 1996),

- no intervention,
- positive intervention (e.g. open discussion, counselling, even promotion),
- punitive action (e.g. reprimand, warning, relocation, job related termination).

The two UK examples provided earlier of the supportive nature of the policies of Brunel University and UCL, are exceptional. Few organisations today exhibit policies to supportively deal with sexually based intimacy in the workplace (Table 2.2). Overall, where specific company policies do exist, they vary considerably in their nature and orientation. Staples, the office supplies retail chain, is reported to have a non-fraternisation policy where a 'personal relationship' between two individuals can lead to resignation and termination of contracts for violation of the company's policy (Cropper, 1997). The Staples policy seems to be particularly concerned with prohibiting managers from having an intimate relationship with a subordinate (Cropper, 1997). Lloyd's of London equally has a strict non-fraternisation policy but with less drastic outcomes. Couples, and others in any relationship that are making the environment less effective, are required not to continue to work in the same area (Welch, 1998).

Delta Air Lines (USA) and Johnson & Johnson had, and have, guidelines regarding the prohibition of supervisor-subordinate dating (Overman, 1998). Others, such as General Motors, have adopted more flexible policies that encourage managers to report romantic affiliations with subordinates in order to reposition formal reporting relationships (Symonds, 1998).

In contrast, other companies are adopting so called 'love contract' policies for supervisor-subordinate relationships. Employers require their employees to contractually disclose romantic attachments in

Table 2.2   Organisational Policies Regarding Workplace Romance

Year	Policies
1984	Mostly focus on nepotism – married couples not to work with or for each other.
1987	Few organisations have written policies concerning workplace romance (only six per cent of Fortune 500 companies).
1994	Informal practice is more common. Seventy per cent of CEO's in a Fortune survey state that work romance is none of company's business.
1998	Thirteen per cent of organisations had a workplace romance policy.
2001	Twenty per cent of survey respondents have written or oral policies concerning romance in the workplace, usually addressing relationships between managers and their subordinates.

Sources: *Business Week* (1984); Warfield (1987); Fisher (1994); SHRM (2001)

return for which they will not be obliged to resign or be transferred. Essentially the 'Consensual Relationship Contract' allows the couple to continue their business pursuits and personal relationship whilst eliminating employer liability in that both parties agree that the relationship is consensual and does not violate the company's sexual harassment policy (Schaefer and Tudor, 2001). Additional emerging evidence supports the continuation of such contracts, as a recent Society for Human Resource Management (SHRM) survey of 558 HR professionals and 663 corporate executives found that 66 per cent of HR and 57 per cent of surveyed executives report that, over the last five years, the greater proportion of employees involved in workplace romances, ultimately marry (SHRM, 2002). Such emerging evidence contrasts sharply with the perceived 'free nature' orientation of Generation X and Y, and much more with the ever greater impinging demands of work. The results of the SHRM survey further suggests that through meeting the demands of work and through not investing sufficient time for social activities, the workplace is becoming a common meeting ground for romantic liaisons (Elder, 1969).

What more to know?

Now, as much as in the past, people's personal and intimate encounters prevail over all other aspects of their life. True, the private and personal lives of the rich and famous attract more attention than that of others less well known. Yet, whether a member of the professions, clergy, politician, public servant or businessman, the secluded and intimate side to these people's lives, poor or famous, continues to attract attention.

So what more do we want to know. Well, for a start, just how pervasive are intimate encounters in the workplace? Who gets involved with whom? How often and to what effect? How do others feel? Should people be left alone to pursue their lives as they wish? Should management intervene and if so – how? Should we create policies and procedures to act as dictates to the personal encounters of others? With so many questions to address, there still remains the most important question to consider, namely, why is such concern and attention given to the intimate relations of ourselves and others? Just some of these queries are addressed in the next chapter.

3
The Study

Bearing in mind the knowledge gained from literature concerning the proclivity, the desired and undesired nature of intimacy in the workplace, a two stage international study of sexuality and intimacy was pursued. First, a number of semi-structured interviews were undertaken in order to explore the intimate experiences of individuals in the workplace. Most of the Stage 1 survey participants gave their permission for the interviews to be taped on the understanding that confidentiality would be maintained. The interviews were transcribed and through categorising key themes and searching for discernable patterns in the responses of the participants, the key issues emerging were identified. Information acquired from these interviews was then used to draft a questionnaire examining the demographic profile of individuals, the culture of their organisation, the nature and level of incidence of workplace intimacy, the repercussions of intimacy and the managerial and organisational policy response to intimacy occurrence. Three pilot surveys were pursued in order to attain the necessary face validity as a prelude to conducting a full survey, namely Stage 2.

Stage 2 involved distributing questionnaires to a random sample of individuals of different status, across varying sectors, working for national and international organisations. Most of the respondents worked for private sector organisations. A smaller number were employed by public service agencies, including a group of middle and senior ranking police officers. A number of questionnaires were returned only partly completed as the respondents found some of the probing questions too intrusive despite confidentiality assurances. Partly completed returns are not included in this report. Overall, 221 individuals fully participated in this survey.

Demographics

Of the 221 respondents, 69 per cent are male and 31 per cent female, with over 80 per cent respondents aged between 21–40 years. Seventy two per cent are caucasian white (British, Irish, American, Canadian, Continental European, Australian) and the rest are of mixed ethnic backgrounds, including Black African, Indian, Pakistani, Chinese and other Asians. Similarly, over 64 per cent identified their religion as Christian based, with a variety of other religions, such as Islamic, Hindu, Hebrew, also declared. A further 16 per cent identified themselves as Agnostic/Atheist. Forty per cent of the sample described themselves as single and 47 per cent as married (Table 3.1). Of those married, 28 per cent report themselves as having remarried and being in their second or third marriage. Irrespective of being married or single, 67 per cent report having parental responsibility for one or more children.

A variety of roles and occupations are represented in the sample, with the greatest proportion in middle and senior management and professional/technical categories (Table 3.2). The professional/technical group includes senior, high paid secretaries as well as specialist information technology (IT) personnel. The management categories also include individuals from sales and marketing, operations and manufacturing, and managers from support service roles such as human

Table 3.1   Marital Status

	Per cent
Married	47
Single	40
Living with partner	8
Divorced	4
Separated	1

Table 3.2   Role Within the Organisation

	Per cent
Middle Manager	35
Professional/Technical	25
Senior Manager	17
Junior Manager	11
Senior Executive	9
Support/Admin Staff	2

resources and finance. Executive directors who may, or may not, hold board responsibilities and non-executive directors of main boards are included in the senior executive category.

Sixty nine per cent of the sample report that they have been in their role for between 1–5 years. However, a greater spread of responses is identified concerning years in the organisation, with 61 per cent of the respondents reporting that they have remained with the same organisation for between 3–10 years (Table 3.3).

In terms of size, a spread of organisations is represented. Twenty four per cent of respondents report their enterprise size as under 250 people and 17 per cent report over 50,000 persons (Table 3.4).

A similar broad spread of distribution applies to the sector background of the respondents ranging from manufacturing, construction, consultancy, finance and retail (Table 3.5). The two categories of 'other services' and 'other' apply to organisations that provide specialist niche services, such as home based nursing care or specialist R & D based organisations, for example, in pharmaceuticals.

The length of working week again induced a broad response, with 40 per cent reporting 45–54 hours and a sizeable 26 per cent indicating they spend more than 55 hours at work (Table 3.6.

Table 3.3   Years in the Organisation

	Per cent
Less than 1	5
1 to 2	19
3 to 5	36
6 to 10	25
11 to 20	10
Over 20	5

Table 3.4   Size – Number of Employees in the Organisation

	Per cent
Up to 250	24
251 to 500	12
501 to 2,500	20
2,501 to 5,000	11
5,001 to 10,000	8
10,001 to 50,000	8
Over 50,000	17

Table 3.5   Sector

	Per cent
Manufacturing/Industrial	15
Manufacturing/Consumer	10
Retail/Wholesale/Distribution	6
Construction	6
Public Sector	12
Financial Services	15
Business Consultancy	8
Other Services	9
Other	19

Table 3.6   Length of Working Week

	Per cent
21 to 34 hours	0.7
35 to 44 hours	34
45 to 54 hours	40
55 hours or more	26

In terms of time spent away from the office and from home, 64 per cent report they regularly travel, whilst 62 per cent equally highlight regularly staying away overnight. Only five per cent indicate that they work from home, thus contradicting the trends identified in the literature review (Chapter 2) of greater home working. In terms of the working environment, 58 per cent report theirs as predominantly male oriented, whereas 40 per cent described theirs as 'a good mix of both' (male/female).

Having outlined the background demographics of this survey, analysis focuses on,

- the nature and context of intimacy,
- the nature of intimate relationships within the workplace,
- intimacy outcomes and impact,
- the impact of IT on intimacy (IT Revolution),
- management intervention in intimacy encounters, and,
- company policy towards employee intimacy in the workplace.

The critical areas emanating from this survey parallel the areas for exploration identified in the review of literature in Chapter 2.

Intimacy: nature and context

Attention is given to examining the nature of intimate and non intimate work relations as well as the job and organisational circumstances (context) within which intimacy occurs. The survey participants, in both Stages 1 and 2 of the study, draw sharp distinction between emotional intimacy and physical intimacy. Emotional intimacy is viewed as a 'close relationship not involving sexual consummation'. Physical intimacy may or may not induce close emotional linkage but does involve physical contact of a sexual nature. The two elements of emotional and physical intimacy emerge as the fundamentally underlying themes throughout this report.

From the Stage 1 interviews, a considerable number of individuals describe their relationships in the workplace as more professional and distant. However, an equally distinct proportion of others emphasise a greater intimacy of interaction, which, for some, has led to physical intimacy. A similar pattern is identified through the postal survey, with 40 per cent of the respondents emphasising low levels of intimacy in their workplace relationships, whereas 39 per cent report experiencing both emotional and physical intimacy or just physical intimacy (Fig. 3.1).

In fact, 60 per cent admit to having experienced some form of physical or emotional intimacy or both. The sharing of tasks and activities

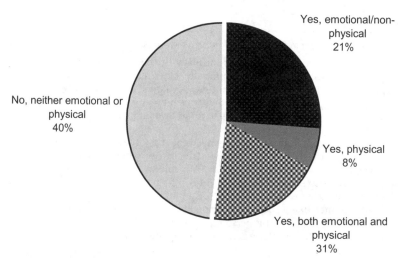

Figure 3.1   Types of Workplace Intimacy

within teams, the team oriented values of the department, the values held by individuals, the needs of individuals, the level of job satisfaction and the overall culture of the organisation, are identified as powerful reasons for virtually two thirds of this sample admitting to some form of intimacy experience at work (Case 2).

Deeper probing of the motivation and needs of individuals highlights that 57 per cent of respondents consider that a powerful driver for continuing to work, or remaining in their current position, is the satisfaction they gain from the social side of employment. The majority of survey participants view themselves as principally being people oriented. The remaining 43 per cent identify themselves as more task, professional, career or money oriented.

In terms of building relationships, 58 per cent report that they form more 'close knit' relations with male and/or female colleagues relatively early into a job or organisation. The reasons given refer to their working style,

It's part of the way I work, otherwise it would be a sterile place.

The two journalists (Case 3) struck a strong friendship as much due to their joint interests as to an inherent dislike of the culture and 'accepted ways of doing things' in their organisation. As the lady journalist admits, it was a friendship at work with little consequence for life outside the workplace. She distinctly differentiates emotional

---

Case 2 *Intimacy, Support and Improvement*

I do not have a 'story' to tell of intimacy in the workplace but, I am experiencing what I feel is an 'emotionally' close relationship which has not been initiated by either person, but has developed as a result of two people of a similar personality/drive trying to achieve the same goals/facing the same difficulties and frustrations with an awareness of the other's needs/ambitions.

This has arisen as a result of my need for support and the other person's willingness to give that support and recognise when support is needed without my asking for it. As a result I am able to accept criticism from this person but also experience distress/hurt if I am occasionally not at the top of their list of priorities (jealousy?). The 'intimate' emotional relationship has led to me talking about this person at home, thinking about this person and wanting to please this person (in a business/emotional sense). As far as personal learning – the experience is 'driving' me at work.

Male Middle Manager, IT Company

Case 3   The Journalist, the Friend and the Divine

Tony and I both worked in junior/middle management in the same department of a large media organisation in the 1980s. However, we were employed in different sections of the department and, in fact, in different buildings of the large campus occupied by the company.

The company context was an intensely emotional one for a number of reasons. As a media organisation, many of the people who worked there were household names and minor celebrities, therefore 'prima donnas'. It was also deeply political, with a great deal of jockeying for position, especially at senior management levels. Many of these Machiavellian manoeuvres were fought out in the limelight. The emotionally charged atmosphere and the fact that many staff members had to work closely together at ungodly hours and away from home around the country and abroad, gave rise to numerous sexual liaisons. Several high profile ones were the cause of various family break-ups.

Tony joined the company about six months ahead of me. Because of our different types of work, our paths crossed only very infrequently, but when they did we discovered that we had a great deal in common. We were in the same age range, married with primary school age children. Neither of us was part of the intrigue of the organisation, although we each interacted with some of the 'personalities' and senior management in the course of our work. This enabled us to observe all these characters at close range and to comment to each other on their 'shenanigans'.

We discovered that our views were in total agreement, and at variance with what would probably have been general opinion around the organisation. We both thought the same people were 'good guys' or 'son of a bitches'. We also had in common the fact that we were both doing part-time postgraduate study. Tony was studying law and I was pursing an MBA. Both of us were doing our courses out of sheer interest and because it was stimulating. However, some people in the company could not understand this. A few of our departmental colleagues resented us for apparently trying to rise above our rightful station in life. These tended to be people who did not have much energy, curiosity or initiative themselves. Other colleagues believed that if we were pursuing further study as a means toward promotion it was a waste of time, since promotion in the company was perceived (correctly) to be largely on the basis of political placement and not on merit or qualifications. Generally, people could not understand that we might actually be studying to learn something, for intrinsic rather than instrumental reasons.

Thus, our agreement on the merits or otherwise of the behaviour of our fellow colleagues and bosses, and our common interests made us confidants, so we would often have long coffee breaks or lunches together. The relationship was always a close collegiate but low profile one. It did not really have much impact on our lives outside work, but was a great source of support in the workplace. Compared to the passion and often histrionics around us, ours would have been seen as a relatively boring friendship.

Thus, it went on for about 3 to 4 years. Then, after a reshuffle and retirement in the department, a promotional opportunity arose in my section and I applied for the position. Naturally, Tony was very supportive and rooting for me. However, when it came to the selection, there was no woman on the interview board, and a manager from another section who had lost his job in the reshuffle was 'fixed up' by having him fill the vacant post. Although I had not expected to get the job, I was still devastated and outraged by the blatant cynicism with which the whole exercise had been carried out. Tony commiserated with me but also observed that there was never any way that someone with my profile was going to get this job, because I was simply not 'one of the boys'. He helped me to see the situation very clearly and to accept that although I enjoyed my job and it was a lot of fun to work in the company, in the long term, I had to be thinking about moving on.

As it happened, around the same time, the university where I had by then obtained my MBA degree, advertised a lecturer job. After conferring with some of the faculty at the university, I was encouraged to apply for the job. Tony was very supportive, although he would miss me if I were to leave the organisation. He told me that his mother had a great gift for prayer and that if she prayed for a favour on behalf of someone, that person usually was granted their wish. Thus, he would get her to pray for me to get the academic job. She was more than happy to include me in her prayers. I might add that Tony and I were both entirely non-religious, but somehow, we still believed in his mother's powers at some level.

So, armed with this divine weapon, I was interviewed for the job, and was informed that I had not been selected, but had been designated as a 'reserve' in case the chosen candidate decided not to take the job. However, the chosen candidate had given a strong indication that he would accept. I later discovered that this candidate had already been doing the job on a contract basis for two years, and had been lined up to get it after an 'official' competition.

So, there I was, again disappointed. Even Tony's mother's prayers had failed, so I must be a hopeless case. Both Tony and his mother (whom I have never met) were most dismayed. Imagine my surprise when about a week later I had a phone call from the Dean of the Faculty of the university, informing me that a second job had opened up, and that the Faculty could offer me this job as a reserve from an existing competition. In fact, I found out that the whole 'reserve' stratagem had been deliberate, since the interview panel was aware that there would be another vacant post due to the imminent departure of a lecturer to another department. They decided that they would use the competition to recruit someone for the advertised post as well as the upcoming one, although they couldn't tell me at the time. So, now Tony's mother was offering prayers of thanks!

Within two months I had left the media organisation. For a couple of years, Tony and I met occasionally for lunch. However, we no longer had the organisational buzz and conspiracy to bind us together. In due course,

Tony himself won a promotion. Eventually, the lunches became less frequent and sometimes cancelled at the last minute due to other pressing commitments. We lost touch, although I heard that he too left the organisation about five years ago and now works in a job where his legal qualification is more useful.

So, I still think of Tony occasionally and wonder how his mother is. Now that I am writing this piece, I am of a mind to pick up the phone or just to send Tony an e-mail message to find out. And maybe ask for a prayer or two.....

Female Irish/American journalist turned academic

intimacy from its physical counterpart, emphasising the supportive and emotionally warm nature of their friendship. The working style element to their friendship is equally pronounced, highlighting the clash between their preferred working style to that predominant in the organisation. However, as seen next, Case 3 supports the finding that 50 per cent of respondents view the culture of their organisation negatively.

- 'I do not like the organisation, but I do get on with the people in this place.'
- 'I like the way teams work around here, but not the culture.'
- 'People count here and that's why I stay.'
- 'Even if not a member of a team, people get on with each other as if they are part of one big team.'
- 'I could get better money elsewhere but I like the way people are treated here.'

As captured in Case 3, the survey respondents report their strong preference for working in small groups or teams.

When exploring the culture of organisations, namely, those attitudes, norms of behaviour and overall conduct shared by most, a broad range of responses emerges (Table 3.7).

The respondents, sub divided into male and female categories, were invited to freely offer their views concerning the culture of their organisation. Such comments as 'male dominated', 'patriarchal', 'male decision makers', 'aggressive', 'very macho', 'men's world', 'clear power structure', 'need for support is perceived as a weakness', are placed in the category of 'masculine'.

Table 3.7 Perception of Organisational Culture

Categories	Representation		
	Total (%)	Male (%)	Female (%)
Entrepreneurial	25	15	10
Fragmented	20	14	10
Supportive	20	12	8
Political	14	8	6
Masculine	8	4	4
Flexible	5	3	2
Resistant to change	4	2	2

The dimension of 'entrepreneurial' represents being 'competitive', 'individualistic', 'swim or sink', 'collection of individuals rather than entity of itself', 'challenging', 'exciting', 'high discretion', 'dynamic', 'combative', 'resource-oriented', 'interesting', 'pragmatic', 'professional', 'performance-oriented', 'knowledge-based', 'robust', or 'hard-working'.

The 'political' dimension is captured through the use of such terms as 'tacit', 'implicit', 'indirect', 'high-context', 'very subjective', 'less powerful have no voice', 'deceptive', 'ambiguous', or 'political undercurrent'. The variable of 'resistant to change' is represented through terms such as 'entrenched in the past', 'resistant to innovation', 'ritualised', 'slow in taking action', 'waiting for crisis instead of being proactive'.

The dimension of 'supportive' is captured through descriptors of 'nurturing', 'comfortable', 'friendly', 'family-like', 'relaxed', 'open', 'social', 'collaborative', happy, nice place to work', 'trusting', or 'good working environment' (see Case 2).

'Cliquish, inner and outer circle', 'many sub cultures', 'fractured', 'aspirational, real and rationalised culture', 'not well integrated', 'in some places supportive', 'held together by personal relationships', or 'star culture' are comments compiled into the category of 'fragmented'. Equally placed in the fragmented category are comments which indicate splits in the organisation, such as 'divided between professional and administrative staff', 'management-support staff divide', or 'management-administrative staff divide'. The descriptor of 'flexible' depicts aspects of 'non-elitist', 'non-hierarchical', or 'flat structured'.

As can be seen, through such open ended analysis, a variety of perceptions concerning the overall culture of the organisation, have emerged. Twenty five per cent of the respondents consider their organisation to be entrepreneurial/market oriented. In contrast 50 per cent take a more negative perspective of their culture, viewing it as fragmented, political, masculine and resistant to change.

However, irrespective of the culture and the fact that certain respondents attribute culture as a possible influence on intimacy occurrence, no discernable relationship emerges concerning the reported incidence of intimacy and 'type' of culture. Bearing in mind that we could not determine all evident relationships between organisation culture and intimacy occurrence, our attention then focused on the individual and their immediate network or peer group.

Concerning the more deeply held values of each individual, an equal scatter of views emerges (Fig. 3.2). Family values are identified as being most important, followed by job related autonomy which is held in equal esteem with the commitment of people to each other (work, social, home related). Also strongly held is the importance of marriage and that it should involve life long commitment. The difficulty in attaining an appropriate balance between home and work life is emphasised, with the impact of work seen as more adversely affecting home life than *visa versa*. Despite the strongly held sentiments concerning the importance of family and the sanctity of marriage, temptation is mentioned by the majority and identified by some as 'succumbing to desire', by others as 'unacceptable pleasures', and alternatively as a powerful learning experience. The perception that people

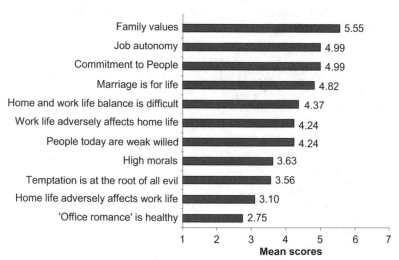

Figure 3.2 Values and Relationships

can be 'weak willed' and will succumb to whatever they find tempting, is balanced by having learnt and matured from a distinctive intimacy encounter as is highlighted in Case 4.

Just as the female senior project manager in Case 4 indicates, she, similar to the greater majority of the respondents, state that they are satisfied with their job. Disaffection with work or the employing organisation does not emerge as a driver for entering into an intimate relationship. Four areas however are identified that are valued most in work; having a job which offers a diverse range of responsibilities and activities; being in a job with broad autonomy and having positive and supportive relations with colleagues, bosses and subordinates; having the discretion to continuously improve one's own professional standards; and being provided with the support and opportunity for development (Table 3.8). Overall, 80 per cent of respondents consider that their career goals and personal objectives are being met in their current organisation through satisfaction of one or more of the above four areas.

The respondents equally identify the circumstances that could 'damage' their present levels of job satisfaction. Diversity not being respected is one critical area. A considerable number of respondents who highlight dissatisfaction with their work, and job in particular, also view their department, or group (of which they are a member), as cult like, instituting conformist behaviour. Lack of diversity within an organisation is considered to accrue through poor recruitment practice whereby senior managers are perceived to appoint in their own likeness. In such enterprises, deviation from tacit, unwritten 'rules', is undesired and, over time, low tolerance for diversity becomes the norm. Those satisfied with their organisation and their work report themselves as consciously broadening their understanding of the nature of the critical and sensitive issues that face their organisation, colleagues and subordinates.

Equally, many also express caution and acknowledge the potential pitfalls that can emerge through pursuing ever greater diversity in

Table 3.8 Job Satisfaction

	Per cent
Diversity	46
Autonomy	26
Social Interaction	26
Security	2

terms of job related practice, social behaviour and thinking. It is recognised that the balance to maintain is between acceptance of personal and social diversities and meeting high service delivery standards. Promoting an image of propriety and service and being publicly exposed for sexual misconduct, attracts scandal. Yet, and as has been displayed in Fig. 2.1 and highlighted in Case 4, irrespective of other considerations, intimacy in the workplace arises.

Nature of relationships at work

In response to the question, 'What are your attitudes towards relationships in the workplace?', the most definitive response to emerge is that intimacy of a physical nature should not occur in the workplace (Fig. 3.3). The most commonly quoted reason is that physical intimacy is disruptive to team working (Case 5).

However, more positive comments are made concerning emotional intimacy. It is recognised that in a supportive working environment it is important for people to share their feelings about their work, their challenges and problems and their perceptions about each other, with each other. In fact, a number of respondents declare that the occurrence of emotional intimacy is healthy in the workplace (Cases 6 and 7).

The relationship outlined in Case 7 emphasises the emotional intensity between the two parties, the reluctance of one of the parties to further progress 'to physical intimacy' and the lack of awareness of the other of the depth of emotion generated. As shown in Case 7 and commented on by most of the survey participants, emotional intimate relationships are viewed as positive, enabling encounters that continue for many years. As highlighted later in this report, encounters of emotional intimacy survive as friendships for much longer periods than those of physical intimacy.

However, many also express that a 'fine line' exists between emotional and physical intimacy. Case 7 draws attention to the fact that only fear of rejection prevented the female student from declaring her affection. Certainly no organisationally centred inhibitions deterred her.

Equally, numerous respondents indicate that when in close friendships, one or other party can misinterpret particular cues thinking that emotional intimacy could be successfully consummated as physical intimacy. The other party however, may not intend to project such signals or may wish the relationship to remain only as emotionally intimate (Case 8).

Case 4   *Feeling Ethical And Still Breaking My Rules*

Question: What key events led to an initiation of an emotionally (and/or physically) close relationship? Who initiated it?

Answer: I had met my husband when I was seconded to do some work for a company that was affiliated to the organisation in which we were both employed. He represented our organisation on the board of the other firm and took me over to introduce me to them. As a consequence of this connection we met occasionally to discuss my work and the business.

It never occurred to me to think of him in any other capacity than as a colleague until one afternoon when we got into a long conversation, following a business meeting. Although we didn't talk about anything personal I felt there to be something intimate in the way we were and I (eventually) left the room feeling both sorry that we'd had to break it up and oddly elated by the time I'd spent with him.

We continued to be friendly as before and he asked me to engage upon a project for him, working again with the affiliated company. We also began to correspond via e-mail, debating minor points of philosophy and semantics, showing off and scoring points off one another. I was having so much fun with this 'flirtation by correspondence' that I didn't realise that I was falling in love with him.

It was when he went away on holiday that summer that it moved into my conscious awareness. I was physically ill from missing him, and fretful, anxious, not eating, not sleeping, unable to concentrate on my work or my home life.

He contacted me by e-mail a day earlier than I was expecting him back from his vacation and suggested that we meet later that afternoon in his office. I found the prospect both exciting and terrifying and could hardly sit still the rest of the day. Actually seeing him again was quite overwhelming and though we sat and talked for over an hour I felt incoherent and tongue-tied. As I left to go home, I reached out and squeezed his shoulder with my hand as I walked past. He smiled but made no other response.

Over the following two or three weeks we spent more and more time together and our flirting grew more overt and more physical; sitting too close; brushing arms; laughing at one another; and I made a habit of touching his shoulder whenever I said goodbye. He never said anything to me about this or reciprocated the gesture.

One evening, as we were sitting working together our fingers entwined and we kissed. This is how the relationship began.

Question: What were the basis/characteristics of emotional and/or physical closeness (e.g. chemistry, physical attraction, love, affiliation, power, dependency, support – emotional)?

Answer: The experience of falling in love was painful and intense. It contained both mutual intellectual respect and a shared sense of curiosity, as well as a strong sexual attraction. Over a relatively short period, we became very close, sharing time and secrets, and the deep bond that developed between us included a strong element of emotional dependency (as it still does).

Question: What impact (if any) did this intimate relationship have on you and/or the group and organisation effectiveness?

Answer: We became lovers six weeks after that initial kiss and we pursued an affair in secret for six months after that. During this time, the organisation was barely affected by our relationship (although I was aware of gossip and speculation surrounding us). Our personal effectiveness in our respective roles was undoubtedly impaired to some extent because our focus was on one another more than it was on our work. We both continued to perform our routine tasks, however, without attracting complaints.

The situation changed dramatically once the affair became public knowledge. Our respective positions within the company (he was the director heading the department in which I worked) threatened the hierarchy of the organisation's structure and left my line manager feeling particularly vulnerable and exposed. Senior management took this very seriously and my lover's position within the organisation was jeopardised.

Three months after the relationship was revealed, we moved in together and, a year later, we were married. We remain quite nauseatingly happily in love. I did, however, leave the organisation soon after he came to live with me. The situation was untenable for me and difficult for him. Following my departure the organisation apparently returned to an even keel – I doubt that this would have been the case had I remained in post.

Question: Personal learning, if any? Was the experience learning/developmental, enhancing of life, traumatic?

Answer: I certainly grew and changed as an individual through this experience. I have learned a lot of things about myself, and about the true nature of love. I have also learned to be more sympathetic and less judgmental of other people (and of myself) when they are facing difficult situations.

Has it enhanced my life? Undoubtedly!

Was it traumatic? Desperately!

Would I take it back? No, not a moment of it.

Question: Any issues that acted as a deterrent to the formation of the intimate relationship (e.g. organisational policy, personal ethical standards, being in a relationship)?

Answer: When he and I met, we were both married to other people and I, for one, had seen enough of the hurt and damage done by infidelity to have sworn to avoid it. I believed myself to be a righteous and ethical person who lived by certain standards and I held to a fairly strict personal code. This relationship broke all my own rules and I ended my former marriage three months after embarking upon the affair because I couldn't live with that deception. The relationship itself is one of profound learning, particularly about mutual trust and support.

Female Senior Project Manager

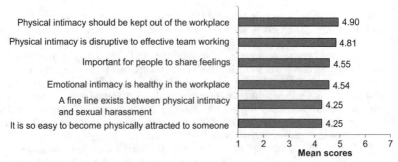

Figure 3.3 shows a bar chart with the following mean scores:

- Physical intimacy should be kept out of the workplace — 4.90
- Physical intimacy is disruptive to effective team working — 4.81
- Important for people to share feelings — 4.55
- Emotional intimacy is healthy in the workplace — 4.54
- A fine line exists between physical intimacy and sexual harassment — 4.25
- It is so easy to become physically attracted to someone — 4.25

Mean scores (scale 1 to 7)

Figure 3.3   Attitudes Towards Relationships at Work

Case 5   Not For Me

Although I have tried to be friendly with people I work with, I have never had, or sought, an 'emotionally (and/or physically) close relationship' with a work colleague – or somebody I have met at work.

My reasons for avoiding an intimate relationship are,

- 'I am married (and have been since the age of 22. I married the day after I graduated).'
- 'I believe that intimacy in the workplace is wrong (both morally – unless both parties are unattached and fully consenting – and in terms of its effect upon efficiency).'

Male Senior Finance Manager, Drinks Company

As emphasised in Cases 7 and 8, despite the strongly held view that physical intimacy should not occur in the workplace, the reasons for the development of physically based relationships at work are identified in Figure 3.4. The primary reason is that of working closely with the other person(s). Through work related proximity, which is likely to involve socialising together, a professional relationship can progress into friendship and/or further into physical intimacy. Certainly, being intellectually, emotionally and physically attractive to the other party, are closely clustered together as reasons for greater intimacy in the workplace. A considerable range of expressions are used to emphasise the mutuality of attraction, such as 'chemistry', 'body language' and 'kindred spirit'. Equally, sharing similar interests and perspectives facilitates a closer working relationship, which, in turn, may become more emotionally and/or physically intimate.

Ranked as less important reasons for the emergence of intimacy are being away from home, dissatisfaction with one's personal life or some

---

Case 6   Not To Be Lonely

The Graduate Scheme I am on is quite unique and so I am not sure it reflects other people's experiences. However, both myself and other individuals on my scheme have found the lack of intimacy quite difficult to cope with. We have spent a year moving around different companies and sometimes spend only a few hours or days with any one person. This makes it difficult to establish any sort of relationship and as someone who is very sociable I have found this hard.

The situation does affect my work/life balance to some extent as often the departments I have visited do take their work relationships away from the office and socialise with colleagues. As I am not really a part of a department or group, I tend to be left out, or back out, of social gatherings. The fact that I have been based in Cardiff, away from my own social circles, has further upset my work/life balance. The balance is not so much to do with time spent on work vs social life, as quality of social life against the intensity of work.

I do not feel that my colleagues or myself have any special requirements or expectations of the workplace. We want to be happy and valued and this is difficult when our role is not very defined and we are constantly moving into new environments. In each new department we are the 'new' person who needs things explained and occasionally we are viewed as spies!

Despite the alienation experienced in the workplace, the graduates have formed relationships with each other and three of us currently live together. This is due to convenience rather than intimacy but it has encouraged a deeper level of friendship. The scheme also offers a mentor scheme, which provides the opportunity to develop a relationship and to discuss any ideas or problems. The mentors tend to be higher management and this makes both arranging any time to see them and forming a truly comfortable relationship difficult.

I would like to see the relationships between graduates encouraged with perhaps the option of a shared household as this would make sense for the scheme. I would also like to see social events and the opportunity for the graduates to meet up regularly to discuss their progress/problems. This is currently possible but only during our weeks at college in pursuit of our management postgraduate qualification.

High Potential Male Junior Manager on a fast track scheme

---

form of dependency need. The survey evidence highlights positive attraction rather than dissatisfaction as reasons for intimacy. The survey results emphasise that intimacy arises because people desire the experience, irrespective of the potentially damaging consequences of sexual consummation and not because they are 'fed up' with their lives.

In Cases 9 and 10, intimacy through prolonged and/or intensive professional interaction is identified as a prime cause of physical intimacy. From there on in, the female divorcee relating her story in

Case 7   The Man of Intellect Who Taught Me That I Had a Heart

Question: What key events led to the initiation of the relationship?

Answer: I was in my early twenties and a new PhD student in a North American university. It was my very first semester at the university. I was desperately trying to survive and possibly distinguish myself in the cut-throat environment of the graduate school. Unlike the other students, I was struggling with the language (being a non-native speaker of English) and with the everyday necessities of life. I was lonely, painfully aware of my inadequacies as a 'scholar' and quite worried about the need to carve a niche for myself in this sterile and rather scary environment.

It was in this context that I was surprised one day to get my very first assignment back with a very high mark and a scribble that looked a lot like it was written in my native tongue. I couldn't believe my eyes. There was no one in the department that I knew of who could speak my language, and, yet, here it was right under my nose, a scribble that was obviously written by the professor in my native tongue. After the class, I talked to my professor and discovered to my amazement that he spent a few months in my home country and was able to speak my language. This ability to converse in my native tongue became the basis for our friendship.

When the time came to select a topic for my PhD research, I decided to go for a topic that I knew he would be happy to supervise. I did it despite the fact that I wasn't particularly interested in that topic myself. I simply wanted to be around him. Once working with him, our relationship became more intimate. We would spend hours discussing issues that were of personal significance to both of us. He told me about his adventures as a new divorcee in a town that he left many years ago and just returned to. I heard about his struggles to stay in touch with his daughter and about his search to establish himself in the university despite stiff competition with his colleagues. He, in turn, was happy to listen to my stories about my life prior to migrating and my plans for the future.

However, there was one topic that we never touched – our relationship. As time went by, I became aware that I was falling in love with him. I found his messages on my desk with the signature, 'Love ... (his name)' disturbing. I found our conversations in my native tongue disturbing too. In fact, at one point, because I wanted to make sure that we got things 'right', I insisted that we speak only in English. At one point or another, I realised that I simply could not think of work with him around, so, while he was away on one of his conferences, I contacted another professor in the department and arranged to do my PhD under his supervision.

When my secret 'love object' returned from his trip, I told him that I was not as interested in my original research topic as I initially thought and that I was going to work with another professor who was an expert in the new area that I was now interested in. To my surprise (and disappointment) he accepted it very well and continued to support me as I struggled to start my new project. He continued to be my 'guardian angel' throughout the whole time that I was in graduate school and never learnt that I was in love with him.

Question: Describe the characteristics of emotional closeness with this man?

Answer: When I think back to the basis for our relationship, I believe that it was a combination of factors. There was definitely a physical attraction. He was the dark, handsome stranger that I always was excited about. Being significantly older than me (he was about 12 years older), made him a sort of a father figure too and his willingness to accept me as an equal was very flattering to my ego. There was also great communication between us and mutual admiration. I considered him the brightest and most interesting man I have ever met and enjoyed our discussions and his obvious respect and trust of me.

However, the most important aspect about our relationship was the emotional rapport that we had with each other. He responded to me on an emotional, unspoken level like no one ever did before. He thought I was the most amazing creature that he ever met and actually gave me a book that had a picture of his favourite actress on the cover, saying that my sensitivity reminded him of her. At the same time, he was totally oblivious to my attempts to get him interested in me sexually. These attempts became quite desperate when I discovered that he was dating another student in the department. I wanted so much for it to be me. And, yet, he barely noticed that I was there as a woman. As far as he was concerned, I was just an amusing, intellectually stimulating friend.

Question: What impact, if any, did this intimate relationship have on you?

Answer: When I consider the impact that this relationship had on me, I can list quite a number of consequences that resulted from it. First, thanks to this man I was compelled to change my research topic and ended up with a topic that was much more fulfilling to me than the original one that I would have done had I not fallen in love with him. Thanks to him, I learnt to appreciate my intellectual abilities in a way that I never did before. It was him who told me once that my questions were the most intelligent he ever heard and I could see his pleasure at attempting to respond to my questions.

My relationship with this man never developed into a full-fledged, sexual one. It was partly because he was not interested and partly because I was afraid to initiate a full-fledged relationship in case I would be rejected. I simply could not conceive of our relationship once he rejected me and preferred not to even try. As the relationship, at the time, never became known (not even to him), it had no impact on anything that happened to me in the graduate school. It did affect my physical health though. As a result of this unrequited love, I ended up developing a life threatening disease and spent a great part of my last year at graduate school in hospital.

When I recovered, I made a pact with myself to let this man know about my feeling towards him even if it got me nowhere. Once out of the hospital, I finished my PhD research and then returned to my home country. Back in my home country, I wrote him a letter in which I told him that I loved him. He responded in one of the most beautiful letters that I have ever received, telling me that he had no idea that I felt that way. For him, he said, 'our relationship was like an island out of time and space'. He told me that he was about to marry the student that he was dating in the past year. I wished him the best of luck and continued to correspond with him for the next twenty years.

Question: What was the outcome of this relationship?

Answer: This relationship resulted in a life long friendship of sorts. After returning to my home country, I met this man face-to-face only once. It was a very amicable meeting. He looked much older and commented (as always) on how old he felt. I told him (as always) that he didn't look old at all ... He seemed to be less than happy in his marriage, but, by this time, had two children and was not about to do anything about it. We chatted about how things would have been if he hadn't married ... He wished me the best of luck on my career and growing family.

It was only many years later that I learnt that he gave his children the exact same names as I had given mine ... It was also many years later that I learnt that he wrote to me on the day that he died. In his last e-mail message, he told me that he was single again. His wife just asked him to leave the family home and he was writing to me, he said, from the office, where he was spending his nights, searching for a new place to live ... I responded by inviting him to visit me, as a guest of honour in my new university. I was amazed that contrary to his usual behaviour, he didn't write back. I was disappointed. It was so much unlike him. It was a few months later that I learnt from reading my alumni newspaper that he died on that same day.

Question: What was your personal learning, if any, from this relationship?

Answer: The most important personal learning that I got from this relationship was not to let issues of 'background' and religion get in the way of my relationships (one of the major reasons that I did not let myself get too close to him was because he was not a member of my ethnic group and religion – I simply could not see myself, at the time, having a relationship with a man 'outside my group'). I also learnt that NOT doing is worse than doing. I simply couldn't forgive myself for not even trying to initiate a relationship with him. When I found myself in similar situations later in my life, I did take the initiative and learnt to live with the consequences. And, yes, the most important learning from this relationship was that I was more than just a brain. This man taught me that I had feelings. It was very much thanks to him that I managed to emerge out of the intellectual cocoon that I created around myself before meeting him and learnt to appreciate that I was more than just a brain. As time went by, and very much thanks to him, I learnt to acknowledge and celebrate my 'feeling self'.

Since this relationship was never 'revealed', not even to the man who was the object of my affections, there were no adverse managerial implications from being involved in it. If at all, I did benefit from it organisationally. Thanks to this man, I was retroactively admitted into a program that I wanted to join, benefited from a number of scholarships that he made me aware of and went on my very first conference, where I presented my very first paper. And, yes, all of these took place without any attempt on his part to initiate a sexual relationship with me ... An interesting reversal of the usual stereotypes...

Female University Professor

Case 8   *Penny Dropped Much Later*

I would like to reflect on a situation that happened 25 years ago but still bothers me somewhat now!!

I attended a full time year long development course in London. There were 13 participants, one was a guy several years older than me. He was black and seemed to have a bit of a chip on his shoulder. I suppose I took him 'under my wing' a bit. He was a few years older than me but compared to the rest of the group we were the youngest by a fair margin.

We were assigned our first teaching practice together. This was in one of London's hospitals so in effect didn't involve being away together. We did get on very well and had lots of heart to hearts! He often said that his marriage was one of convenience and that he didn't love his wife. I had been married about 4 years and was happy and quite settled. My husband and I had quite a lot of trust between us, he had female friends and I had male friends. It was no big deal.

The third teaching practice was back in the institution that had seconded me. This chap arranged through a variety of means to come to my place of work. He, I found out later, lied to get a placement to be with me. I was quite accommodating, showed him the area, and invited him home for meals and we spent days at the coast together. I thought I was doing the hospitable thing for a colleague! It never crossed my mind it was anymore than friendship!

He then got a job in the same place where I worked, which included moving 250 miles south for himself and his wife. We worked together for several months and then one afternoon when we were alone and not busy, I can remember it was a Wednesday, he suggested we went home to his house and 'did what we both had been waiting for ages'. I was so surprised and went all prudish.

After that we hardly spoke, apart from him being incredibly angry with me, and saying that I was not honest or genuine and had led him astray. Apparently to other people it had all been totally obvious to the extent that when I left several months later, on maternity leave, they thought the truth would all be revealed when the baby was born!

I still feel bad about this, because I was so naïve, didn't see what everybody else did and in some ways felt guilty because he had uprooted his life in the North and put his career backwards as the institution I worked at was not as prestigious as where he had left. To add to this, when he accused me of not being genuine, it took me about 10 years of reflection for the penny to drop as to what he meant.

Consequently I have since been really careful not to give out mixed messages, but I have also recognised that through my career I have worked much better with male managers because mostly the chemistry has been a factor in the working relationship which has added enjoyment to the everyday job.

Female Physician

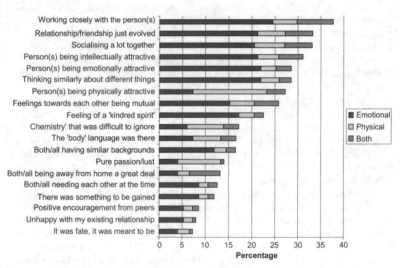

Figure 3.4 Reasons for the Development of Relationships in the Workplace

Case 10 highlights that the success or damaging consequences of the relationship are partly attributable to the maturity of the two parties involved and the attitude and policies adopted by the organisation. Unlike the female professor of Case 7, the divorcee in Case 10 mentions her company's intimacy policies indicating her consciousness of such potential inhibitors.

Case 9   Clever, Attractive and in Service

Case study analysis of one internationally renowned consulting organisation revealed that up to 59 per cent of males and females interviewed experienced physically intimate relationships in the workplace during their career (Table 3.9). The organisation is publicly well known, charges high fees, and attracts high quality clients. In order to provide a high level of service, well qualified professionals who are experienced and socially adept people, are hired. Poor performing personnel are not tolerated and leave. In this organisation, gender is an insignificant consideration concerning the occurrence of physical and emotional intimacy as over 80 per cent of those interviewed report experiencing emotional and/or physical intimacy.

Table 3.9   Experience of Physical Intimacy

Gender	Experience (%)	No Experience (%)
Male	35	26
Female	24	15
Total	59	41

Although the reported intimacy experience in this consulting organisation is higher than the average emerging from the rest of this survey (Fig. 3.1), the reasons given for intimacy arising are similar, namely, work related proximity, availability, similar interests and desires and the choice to do so. Similar to the survey results, realisation (or not) of a person's job objectives or levels of job satisfaction are found to be unrelated to people's proclivity to enter into physically intimate relationships.

The one consistent reason given for the higher incidence of physically intimate relationships occurring in the consulting organisation in comparison to the survey average is, the level of intensity of project work and teamwork. Consulting assignments involve small teams working intensely together for limited periods of time on behalf of a client. The requirement to meet project goals within a specific timeframe, according to the contract agreed with the client, increases the intimacy of working relationships. Consultants spend more time together, at times not going home for two or three days so as to meet assignment deadlines. In order to work well together, the interviewees strongly emphasise the 'need to know each other better'. Thus, greater collegiate intimacy, for sound professional reasons, is viewed as two steps away from physical intimacy. That additional step is desire and the final step is conscious choice. Those that desire further intimacy report that they take that next step. Those that do not, do not!

International Consulting Organisation

Case 10   Divorced, Dating and Delectable

After my divorce, I was fortunate to be working for a large division of a computer company. Our facility housed production, as well as a large group of R&D staff – predominantly male, many of them single and in a reasonable age bracket for me to consider dating material. The company policies only prohibited personal relationships when one person was in a direct reporting relationship to the other. Two people from different departments need not hide the fact that they were involved outside the workplace.

The company also had a number of organised – yet extremely amateur – athletic activities. For example, there was a co-ed softball league and several indoor soccer teams. These served as convenient venues for getting to know people within a group before individual dating.

I had been with the company for more than five years when Mack started working in another department. I first got to know him as a co-worker. Our job required frequent interaction. We both began spending time with a group that gathered at company-sponsored events and frequently the entire group spent time together before and after.

For quite some time I knew I was interested in exploring more of a relationship with Mack. Mack later told me he was very interested too, but not sure I was. So, it's a little difficult, looking back, to describe exactly how things moved forward. It seems we gradually shifted into an intimate relationship but without ever going through the formality of a first date.

Before then, I had already made certain decisions about how to handle casually dating people I knew from my workplace, but I could see this was going to be much more than two or three dates. I did give additional thought to how I would deal with seeing him at work some day, if there had been an argument the night before – or even the potential of an eventual break up.

Some of my comfort level came from my impression of how he would handle these things. We first met as professionals; now we had added on an additional relationship. If the added dimension was taken away, I really thought we would be able to return to the original professional relationship. As the relationship progressed, Mack showed a clear ability to interact daily on work issues the same as always. Having myself been through the break up of a 16-year marriage, I knew I was capable of ending a relationship without becoming vindictive or airing my emotions in public. In the case of my former marriage, there was a need to maintain civility for the sake of my son. With Mack, should things not work out, there would be need to do the same for the sake of our professional responsibilities. It can be done.

I will admit, though, that I had never understood how people could have a long-term personal relationship and work together day after day. Dating Mack was the first time I had been able to see myself in that situation, and I felt surprisingly comfortable with it. I even felt it was an advantage that we had been co-workers first. I felt a certain security that we would always be equal partners in our personal relationship, because we had started out knowing each other as equals in another setting.

I could have been wrong. I'm sure many people have started out with the same feelings of security and hopeful expectations, and later found themselves embroiled in dreadful break ups that carried into the working environment to the detriment of those two individuals as well as others working around them. My assumptions were never fully tested. Within a year, I left the company for another job. However, I've always felt that Mack and I were better able to share work issues, both stressful events and special successes, because we each understood the other in that environment – more so than people who have never worked together.

I'm looking back on this now after 20 years with Mack, so we never did face the break up situation. Of course, things weren't always smooth sailing, but we are still together and plan to stay that way. Still, I wouldn't recommend a workplace romance to everyone. I can see that I would not have been able to deal with it as well at an earlier time in my life. Also, it would be much riskier to initiate in a working environment where the interim social interaction is not so readily available.

I don't have any magical guidelines to ensure success. My only advice would be to honestly think through the day-to-day implications and make sure you want the whole package – the possible benefits and the recognisable risks. People today spend so much of their lives at work that it has become the primary opportunity to meet others with compatible values and interests. I don't think we can expect relationships to not develop. And sometimes they work out just fine and sometimes not!

Female Senior Computer Manager

The survey respondents also volunteered information on the nature of their physical intimacy experience. The greatest incidence of intimacy, of an emotional and/or physical nature takes place with a member of the opposite sex (Fig. 3.5). The greater number of intimacy partners are colleagues, mostly in the same department or a colleague in another department or unit (as in Case 10). In the minority of cases, intimacy is reported with a member of the same sex, with the majority reporting emotional but not physical involvement (Friskopp and Silvestein, 1995).

The two lowest reported intimacy experiences are with subordinates or bosses. With subordinates, a greater incidence of physical intimacy is reported than those with the boss. The most common occurrence is between manager/secretary and/or team leader with team worker. One reason for the low response in the subordinate to boss related category is that in this survey most respondents held middle/senior manager and professional status than that of junior/manager, support staff or operative. As more 'bosses' completed the questionnaire than subordinates, the sample is skewed. Had more secretaries for example, participated in the survey, the results could have been different.

Concerning the personal status of the individuals involved in physical intimacy, the majority report themselves as single (Fig. 3.6). Interestingly, whether both parties are single, one single/other married, or both married, the reported levels of emotional intimacy are comparable. The difference is migrating from emotional intimacy to physical intimacy, a proclivity that is, by far, more experienced by two partners that are both unmarried.

Respondents who took part in both Stages 1 and 2 of the survey, highlight the nature of the inhibitors to conducting emotional and physical intimacy in the workplace (Fig. 3.7). The greatest reported inhibitor is each individual's personal values and beliefs, with each person choosing their level of involvement in either emotional and physical intimacy, or both. People do not report being overwhelmed

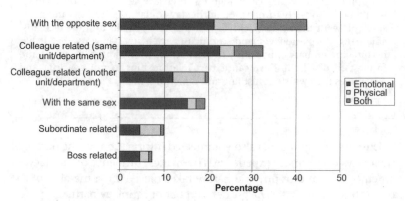

Figure 3.5 Intimacy Experience; with Whom?

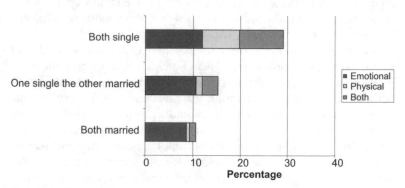

Figure 3.6 Personal Status

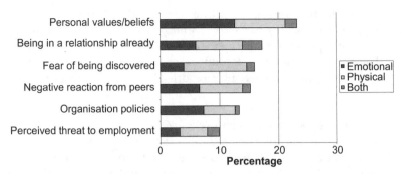

Figure 3.7 Inhibitors to Relationship(s) in the Workplace

by circumstances or being 'bowled over' by pressure from others to pursue a relationship, or by the culture of the organisation or even team spirit. The respondents admit that what they pursue or take no further, is their decision. Also, being in an already established relationship and the fear of being discovered are additional inhibitors. In particular, fear of being discovered is identified as the more powerful inhibitor of physical intimacy. Additionally, expected negative reaction from peers is, for some, an influential brake on both emotional and physical intimacy. The two least inhibiting forces to pursuing emotional and/or physical intimacy in the workplace are the responses by the organisation. Although ranked low, the tacit, (i.e., understood) or explicitly visible policies that the organisation pursues, or is perceived to pursue, are viewed as equally inhibiting of emotional and physical intimacy. Threat to employment is perceived as far more inhibiting to physical than emotional intimacy.

Intimacy outcomes and impact

Those directly involved

Stage 1 interviewees and Stage 2 survey respondents offer their views concerning the impact of intimacy encounters and distinguish between intimacy outcomes at a personal level and at an organisational level.

At the personal level, the greatest benefit from an intimate experience is that of friendship (Fig. 3.8 – see Case 7). Terms such as 'sharing', 'understanding', 'non-judgemental support', 'pleasurable experience', 'gain through the relationship', 'excitement', 'challenge' and 'fun', are repeatedly adopted. In fact, 'fun' is noted as the second most positive outcome. Further, a considerable number of respondents identify that relationships, of either emotional and/or physical intimacy, are still ongoing (see Cases 3 and 7). Thus, the greater majority of intimacy encounters are experienced, or recalled, in a positive light.

The female consultant's account of her relationship (Case 11) captures the majority of experiences reported by the survey respondents, namely that,

- both parties benefited from the experience,
- both parties held comparable/similar status in the organisation,
- both parties eventually went their separate ways,
- one or both parties held positive memories of the encounter,
- management and the rest of the organisation had little or no knowledge of the incidence of physical intimacy,
- the need to work closely together led to physical intimacy.

The contrast to the majority of the survey respondents is that the female academic turned consultant was married and living with her husband at the time of the affair.

Whether heterosexual (Case 11) or homosexual (Case 12), comparable positive recollections of physical intimacy emerge. The encounters, whether they continued as a longer sustained relationship or not, are viewed as significant positive experiences, which, despite any initial trauma, led to a better life, apart or together!

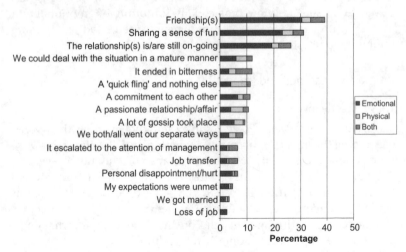

Figure 3.8   Outcome of Intimate Relationship(s)

Case 11 The 'Fly by Night' Who Taught Me About Courage

Question: What key events led to initiation of the emotional/physical relationship? Who initiated it?

Answer: I was in my mid twenties and on my very first year of teaching in a USA regional university. I was back in my home country after spending a few years overseas getting my PhD degree. It was a very difficult year of adjustment to a new environment. In addition to struggling with a budding academic career that didn't seem to go anywhere, I was also embroiled in a difficult marriage in which I felt unloved and misunderstood. My passion, at the time, was my involvement with the feminist movement. I was busy organising consciousness-raising groups for young women in my home town and writing articles for the local media about feminist issues.

It was at this point that I was approached by some of my students at the university and asked if I would agree to participate in an open debate about the role of women in society. I was to represent the female perspective while another faculty member, that I had not met yet, was to represent the male perspective. I agreed enthusiastically. A few days later, I met my 'opponent'. I was fascinated by this man. He was unlike any other man that I had met. His work at the university was a side-activity for him. His major activity was being a management consultant and organisational development expert, which was exactly the career that I wanted to switch into.

Instead of preparing for our public debate, I found myself listening to him and being inspired by his stories about his work and his life. By the time that we finally had our public debate, the sexual tension between us was palpable. In fact, instead of talking about the conflict between the sexes, as we were supposed to do, we found ourselves presenting quite a 'united front' that the audience found surprising and probably disappointing.

When our public debate ended, we spent the rest of the evening discussing our private lives. It was a passionate night that did not end with a full sexual encounter but was passionate enough to make me 'confess' to my husband a few days later that I had an interest in another man and was keen to explore a relationship with him. Shortly afterwards, I moved to live with my mother. At that point in time, I met with my new lover and we 'consummated' our affair for the first time.

Our relationship was short but significant in that it inspired me to eventually divorce my husband and move to another city where I launched a new career as an organisational consultant. This was quite a change from the sheltered 'good girl' life style that I led up until then.

One of the most inspiring conversations that I had with this man was when I told him that I wanted to become a consultant but didn't feel that I had all the necessary qualifications. He stopped me in my tracks and said, 'You have a PhD and this is all the formal education that you will ever need. The rest, you will learn by doing as you go ...' This was the very first time that anyone told me that I was good enough to do anything, absolutely anything, and not just in the intellectual area but in ANY arena. It was one of the most liberating moments of my life and I will always be grateful to this man for making it happen for me.

As I said, our relationship did not last long. Within a few months, I became aware that he continued to date other women and did not consider our relationship 'exclusive'. This was not a situation that I was willing to accept. Since I did not see any way of 'reforming' him, I let him drift out of my life. Still, I did not let this setback stop me from continuing with my divorce and the transition into a new career. Despite the fact that he, my inspiration, was no longer part of my life, I continued to pursue my personal goals without him. I did hear from him years later. He was still drifting in and out of relationships and in and out of careers, but we never met again.

Question: What were the characteristics of emotional closeness?

Answer: The basis for this relationship was definitely chemistry or physical attraction. This man was a 'hunk', an attractive guy who was fully aware and very proud of his physical attractiveness to the other sex. At the same time, he was also highly intelligent and able to 'play' with ideas and inspire interesting thoughts in everyone around him, including me. I remember in particular his statement, which I pondered for years, 'There is nothing more logical than emotion and nothing more emotional than logic.' I also remember him telling me that, 'True love means that you want more than you need rather than need more than you want.' At the time, the mere fact that one could sit and debate the meaning of concepts such as 'love', 'logic' and 'emotion' was a revelation to me. It was so refreshing ... I simply basked in the freedom that this man exuded and enjoyed every minute of being around him.

There was no power or dependency involved in our relationship. He was a free spirit and was not interested in me being tied to him. I was not interested in having him tied to me either. While I had a secure job in the university, he was an outsider, so he could not affect my life at work in any direct way. As for emotional support, there was very little of it ... He was not the type to get attached emotionally to anyone. In retrospect, I think of him as a confused man, who I met at a difficult time in his life. He just got divorced and was flexing his muscles in the dating arena while at the same time trying to meet his obligations as a father ... But I, at the time, did not see him as that. To me, he was an exciting hero who presented me with a model for life. He came into my life at a time that I was ready to be liberated and changed it forever.

Question: What impact (if any) did this intimate relationship have on you?

Answer: The major impact that this relationship had on me was that it led to the ending of my marriage and the beginning of my new life as a single woman. Once I met this man and even before our relationship became sexual, I felt compelled to tell my husband about it. This ended our marriage. My husband was shattered by my confession and I saw no other choice but to move out.

The upheavals that resulted from this move and the eventual ending of my marriage disrupted my career quite significantly. But then I was already convinced, even before I met the new man, that I wanted my marriage to end and I wanted to start a new career as a management consultant. So, what may have seemed as a disruption, was not perceived by me as such. When I eventually moved to another city where I could pursue my new career, it was with much enthusiasm.

As for my marriage, even though the new relationship did not result in a marriage or even a long term friendship, I cannot say that it resulted in a trauma or big disappointment. I considered this man as one who played an important role in awakening me to the possibilities that lied outside the life that I had up until my meeting with him. He liberated me from a pattern that I wanted to break. He inspired me to pursue my dreams. How could I be angry at him for that? And, yes, since the relationship was short lived, it didn't have any long-term implications on my life at work.

Question: On reflection, was the experience enhancing, traumatic, developmental?

Answer: This relationship was definitely inspiring and enhancing. Where else other than work could I have met a man who had values so different from mine and who, thanks to his values, could get me thinking differently about my life in and out of work? I was at a crossroad in my life. I was unhappy with both my marriage and my work life, and yet, I didn't have the courage to do anything about it. I was a product of a marriage (my parents) where both partners had never taken big chances with their lives. My father spent his whole life working in the same job for the same (very secure) company. My mother spent most of her adult life as an employee of one single organisation. Both my parents could not be a role model to me in terms of encouraging me to leave my marriage, move to another city or start a new career, as none of them ever dared do any of these. In fact, once I was back from doing my PhD overseas, my parents expected me to settle down, have children, and spend the rest of my life in my home town. It was this 'fly-by-night' lover who gave me a taste of a different kind of life that was less secure and much more rewarding. It was he who was my role model to a different kind of life. Even though, I probably wanted him to be 'just mine', once I realised that he was in my life to play a short but very important role, I found it in my heart to forgive him and be grateful to him.

In addition to the work related learning, I also learnt some important personal lessons from this relationship. It was the very first time that I allowed myself to pursue a relationship that was based solely (or mostly) on physical attraction. It was also the very first time that I allowed myself to 'fall in love' with a man who was clearly not the marrying type. In fact, this man was the absolute opposite of the 'serious type' that I have been attracted to before I met him. Being around this man taught me that sexual attraction was not necessarily a guarantee for sexual compatibility (there was very little sexual compatibility between us). It also taught me that even though I could fall in love with a man who did not have a need to be 'exclusive', I had the strength to move on with my life once I became aware of this fact. Contrary to other people who found themselves in such relationships and became 'trapped', I ended the relationship once I heard from this man that he did not intend to be loyal to me. The knowledge that I had the strength to do it remained with me as possibly the most important lesson that I learnt from this relationship. And yes, perhaps the most important lesson that I learnt from this man at both the professional and personal level was about courage. Thanks to him, I discovered that I was a courageous woman who was capable of doing things that I had no role models for. His example and the lessons that I learnt through him remained an inspiration for me for many years to come.

Question: Did management or others in the organisation know of this relationship?

Answer: Because this relationship did not last long, was mostly clandestine, and did not take place at the university, it did not have any impact on my status at work. Management was not aware of this relationship at any time and did not have any reason to take any action about it.

Senior US Female Consultant

Negative experiences of intimacy are also identified through the survey but these are noted as considerably less influential and important to the individual(s) than those recalled as positive (Fig. 3.7). Even then, positive comments also cluster with the more negative perspectives. From the rank ordering of outcomes, the trend to emerge is that the greater the level of physical intimacy, the marginally greater level of negative experiences, with some describing the relationship as ending in acrimony, bitterness, separation, accompanied by unwelcome gossip in the workplace. Others are more neutral in their description, emphasising their attempts to manage their circumstances by creating 'clear water' between professional and personal relationships (Case 5). For others, the physically intimate relationship is seen as a 'quick fling' that petered out. Certain comments refer to personal disappointment in the sense of unmet expectations, or a negative organisational response. A small minority report that their emotional and/or physical intimacy experience in the workplace led to the couple marrying (Case 10).

At the organisational level, attention focuses on the costs of the relationship (Table 3.10).

The greatest proportion of responses are placed in a broad category, labelled general negativities, due to the wide spread of responses. The costs for the organisation include, 'spent too much time talking to

Case 12 Recollections of a Gay Man

I was a qualified audit senior for a firm of accountants in the UK whose client was an internationally renowned personality with a company based in a remote tax shelter. It was my job to take an assistant for a week and review the accounting records for tax and investor purposes.

A relatively straightforward job although I had been forewarned that the accountant had not yet completed the final accounts of the company for me to review.

In those days my boundaries were very clear about sex and intimacy and work and they should never be crossed. I was in an eight year long relationship which had been successful and fulfilling. On reflection I could point to the seven year itch as the reason for what unfolded but at the time I had no idea what I was about to walk into.

Yes, I got off the plane and walked into the client's office to find his accountant waiting to meet me. Yes, to me he was stunningly good looking and I made a mental note to be extra careful. I had no idea that he was gay. Any false signal or unguarded comment would be detrimental to client relations and I was about to leave the firm I was working for and wanted a reference, which I knew, was going to be exceptional. I did not want anything to change that.

I found the accountant, very amenable and his voice mellifluous. Every debit and credit was spoken as if it was the next tasty morsel over a seductive dinner. And yes, he was very attentive and hospitable ensuring that my colleague and I were taken out to dinner each evening. This guy was fantasy material. I was busily tending to my assistant, who I found out years later was also gay and knew exactly what was going on, but ensured that he gained the best experience and modelling by a senior audit manager on how to work with the client. I was managing a job outside of the home country and providing review and feedback of my assistant's work and at the same time managing the time costs for the job against the previous year's audit experience. The pressure was on and I was performing well, aided by the frissant that existed between the client's accountant and myself. I didn't stop to analyse the emotional content of the situation. I was working and spoke to my life partner each evening who was working in England and preparing to move jobs down to London so that we could live together.

By Thursday it was quite clear that the client would not be able to complete the work I needed to review by the weekend and it was agreed that I would stay a further week and my assistant would be sent home. I felt some discomfort at this and a certain failure because the profession is highly competitive, even within the same firm, year on year, with employee's work and time cost.

Friday night came and I put my assistant on the plane back home. I felt relieved that I didn't need to deal with him any longer and now I could concentrate on the job in hand. I had been given the company apartment for my stay, which was a glamorous suite of rooms overlooking an extravagant terrace. I was beginning to detach from reality and move into a cinematic existence. Pier took me out to dinner, then to the expatriate club to experience the crushing boredom and soulless existence of life away from England and finally, drunken and laughing we arrived at the apartment and a nightcap. Coffee in the kitchen turned into the drunken grope, the passionate kiss and a night of lovemaking. Hey, I was away from home and living a dream with someone who was full on and wanted me, no negotiation was required.

The impact was clearly one of constructive performance. At no time was my professional life compromised and I still felt that I could report irregularities if they were uncovered. Despite the passionate affair I was still dedicated to my work during working hours.

The outcome was a secret affair for a further four months, with skiing weekends and Christmas parties. At the end of this time I separated from my partner and we became an item, which lasted for six years.

The learning for me was traumatic. How could I have been so dedicated to a relationship of eight years and then to have it completely overturned in such a short space of time? I realised that I hadn't expressed to my partner of eight years some of the resentments that had built up over the time of our relationship and somehow the passionate affair enabled me to cash in all of my resentment and start afresh. It was only at the end of this relationship that ran for six years that I began to fully understand the emotional hooks and the psychology between us that had enabled what turned out to be a turbulent and destructive relationship.

I left the firm I was working for six weeks later without anyone knowing what had happened. Even one year later the Audit Partner mentioned my now new life partner without any awareness that we were living together as a couple.

The report I filed at work was complete and accurate and considered a job well done.

Senior Auditor

Table 3.10 Intimacy Impact on Group and Organisation Effectiveness

Impact	Per cent
General negativities	35
No impact	22
Conceal affair	17
Trust/Defensive	14
Performance	12

each other', 'shifted focus on each other rather than work', 'the organisation invested in me but did not realise full return', 'disruption generally and negative effects on work, team and even department or organisation reputation'. However, the overall conclusion to draw from the impact of intimacy arising from 'general negativities' is one of irritant rather than serious problem.

In contrast, reputation loss is viewed as having more damaging consequences. The impact on the organisation due to reputation loss correlated positively with the status and level of individuals in the organisation. Those holding chief executive or chairman roles potentially inflict substantial reputational damage to the organisation as a result of an intimacy encounter becoming public. As a result, 17 per cent of respondents report the lengths they have gone, or would go, to conceal their affair, which include hiring private detectives to undermine the credibility of the other party, and/or teams of lawyers to prevent the media and press from 'capturing' the story.

However, 22 per cent of respondents report no impact on the organisation, or the performance of the team, or other potentially interested parties. A particularly frustrating experience for those involved in an emotionally and/or physically intimate relationship is that they feel the need to pretend that no such relationship exists when personal and organisational performance is not impaired or unlikely to be impaired.

As Case 13 highlights, the efforts some people go to to conceal their relationship is directly connected to their growing disrespect for the organisation, first because of the felt intrusion into their lives and second, because such caution is viewed as unnecessary. As shown in Table 3.10, the views of Jeremy and Pauline (Case 13) are supported by 22 per cent of respondents. However, unlike Jeremy and Pauline, many of this 22 per cent group report they do not attempt to conceal their relationship. Their attention to the task is high and their sense of professionalism is respected by colleagues. Even though others know of their intimate encounter, work relationships in the group or department are reported as not damaged or undermined.

In contrast, a minority (13 per cent) of individuals involved in an intimate relationship admit to a drop in performance on their part, or for having stimulated defensiveness in others, which, in turn, has organisational implications.

- 'We were both seen in a different light.'
- 'We tended to be over protective to each other and that irritated others.'
- 'Depends on each event and context. Here people gossip and that's the real problem. However, when a power relationship is involved, that causes disturbance in the team. You do not know what is said to whom and that can seriously damage trust.'

Case 13   *Pretending for Social Events*

Two professionals in their late twenties, working in an international law practice, described the lengths they went to conceal their relationship. The two parties involved are Jeremy, a psychologist, who held the position of senior human resources manager and Pauline, a lawyer, who joined the practice the year before.

Jeremy: 'They have this really old fashioned idea about personal relationships at work – you can't have them or, if you do, you are out!'

Pauline: 'It's crazy. There must be about five or six other couples, all like us, trying to hide their affair. The reason the management do not know is that everybody here is very professional. They do their job as required and more!'.

Jeremy: 'What is irritating and wastes time is what we have to do to conceal our relationship, pretend we are distant from each other, not speak to each other at work; be careful where we are seen socially outside of work. That is irritating, to think that management here figuratively follow you when the work is done.'

Pauline: 'As if we have a social life! We both work over 60 hours per week. Do you know how long it really takes to achieve 30 client billing hours – virtually twice that. And Jeremy, in dealing with all the people problems here, he is late into the night at least three times a week. On average, he works longer than me.'

Jeremy: 'Probably the most irritating experiences of all are the social occasions, the Christmas party, the leaving do's. We both turn up as single people. The others bring their partners. One or two bosses have already commented that both of us should find someone. One of the partners tried to introduce me a divorcee friend of his, ironically right in front of Pauline.'

Pauline: 'That really pissed me off!'

Jeremy: 'And all this deceit for what? People have relationships at work. Here, in particular, nobody knows. In other places nobody could care less. Work is not affected. In some places there may be a little bit of gossip, but basically nobody could really care less. The only ones affected are us. As soon as I can leave, I will. What a waste. They have paid for me to be trained and yet I will be off as soon as I can and all for what? – an outdated Victorian, irrelevant, morality.'

Psychologist and Lawyer

Third party involvement

How do colleagues, subordinates and bosses react to the intimate relationships of others? Attention is given to exploring the effect of intimate relationships on others in the workplace and their view concerning how the intimate relationships of others affect their own individual, group and organisation effectiveness. The greater majority highlight that others' intimate work related relationships have no impact on them or the performance of others (Fig. 3.9; Case 14).

As highlighted in Case 14, no one complained, hence no issue. Further exploration did show that most in that department knew of the relationship and approved. Both the man and woman involved were highly respected and also genuinely 'liked' as people. The fact that intimacy occurred within a military infrastructure seems to have been irrelevant to the outcome.

Only 29 per cent of the respondents emphasise that they personally, the team/department of which they are a member, or the organisation, has been affected and even then, the most commonly reported reaction is that of feeling awkward (Fig. 3.10).

- 'I and others are uncomfortable. Their affairs send out negative signals. People can see his family is suffering.'

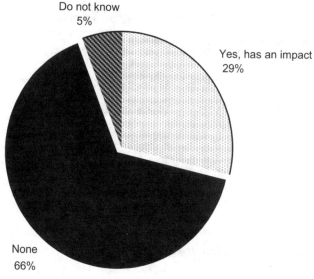

Figure 3.9 Impact of Other Peoples' Relationships

Case 14   Intimacy in the Military

Our working environment is rather diverse in relation to gender, for uniform and civilian personnel both from the UK and the USA. I think that is great although my team was composed of only male staff until recently. This is particularly significant as after 20 years my marriage broke down. I went through a really rough time for a couple of years until a new female member entered my team. A civilian colleague suggested that I should become more acquainted with this new arrival as she seemed to display similar interests. I did not pay much attention until months later, when one day, over lunch, I mentioned to my team that I was contemplating taking a skiing trip in the Alps. Jane, the only woman in my team, started giving me skiing tips and suggested places to go and visit. That was the very first time that I looked at her as a woman and not as a member of the team. Over time, our conversations became more frequent as we both discovered that we shared the same passions. That was a year ago. Now we live together. She and her two children have moved in with me. When Jane finds an alternative post within the department, we shall announce our engagement. I think everybody knows that we are a 'pair' but they are not confronting the issue as we both behave very professionally.

Male Senior Officer, Ministry of Defence

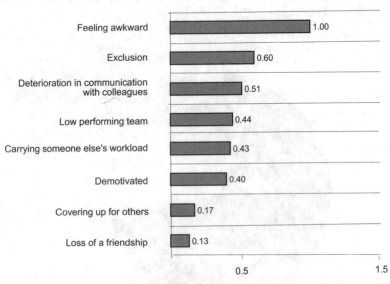

Figure 3.10   Affect of Intimate Relationship on Self

- 'Had no effect on me but may have effect on the organisation; people cannot focus on their proper job – too much distraction.'
- 'Reduced efficiency, as group and organisational effectiveness is based on professional relationships rather than preferential relationships.'

In examining the comments made supporting the ratings captured in Figure 3.9, for many, the feelings of awkwardness, on reflection, are viewed as uncomfortable but not important. Namely, the individual experienced the intimacy relationship of someone else as a considerable problem, but on consideration, it had only a marginal impact on individual or their and their team's ways of working.

Critical is the difference between feelings of awkwardness and a discernable impact on performance. Of the few that report serious concern with the intimacy of others, the damage to the performance of the individual and team/unit in terms of exclusion of information and deterioration in communication is emphasised.

- 'It was most disruptive. She was more junior to him. When nobody knew, they gossiped to her about him and when they found out she was with him, not only did nobody trust her, people did not know who to trust. Communication between us became non existent.'
- 'It is difficult to deal with either one individually. One of them is in a power position. Comment, information, views made by others gets reported back to one of the two. I must be careful with them.'
- 'It was a fairly open team. Now that she has his ear, and by the way, I do not think they are having an affair, but he seems besotted with her. Nobody dare say anything. What's worse, he was a pretty good team leader. Now, he checks everything out with her first. We talk to each other in small cliques. Nothing of significance is said at team meetings and what is more, we do not know what information we should know more about! She edits out what she does not want others to hear. Being in a state of not knowing what you do not know, is bad!'

The survey highlights that performance deterioration and damaging communication particularly occurs when emotional and/or physical intimacy arises in a power imbalanced relationship, namely that between boss and subordinate. The combination of feeling excluded with trust and communication deteriorating, are the experiences identified that harm team performance. At the level of the individual undertaking particular tasks, most report that they continue to perform as well as before any intimacy relationship emerged. It is at the team level that both morale and the motivation to improve performance, as a unit, is undermined. Most report discomfort in raising issues that are necessary to debate in terms of team morale and performance. Those survey respondents who report high levels of discomfort state that in order for the discussion to be meaningful, the reasons for the deterioration of morale and how to go about improving performance requires naming particular individuals which, in turn, is likely to offend either party in the intimate relationship.

- 'The male performed poorly. The female performed well but passed information onto him. She made it very difficult for me.'
- 'For me, I get on with both A and B. However, if anyone upset A, then B got upset too. Many in the team had to influence A and B outside the meeting in order to facilitate more favourable decisions in the meeting. I can tell you, effectiveness really suffered.'

Only on a few occasions was favouritism for one of the parties in an intimate relationship reported. Case 15 is exceptional in that a transfer of responsibilities further complicated an already tense situation. However, similar to other reported circumstances individual and team morale was considerably damaged. Further, negative impact occurs when individuals feel they need to 'cover up' for someone else's relationships, distort the truth or make choices that ultimately damage a friendship, or previously sound collegiate relationships.

- 'It affected me negatively as I was implicated. I had to make moral decisions that were difficult. It cost me the friendship of a good colleague.'

However, as with favouritism, 'covering up' for others and loss of friendship emerges only in a small minority of cases.

On being asked to summarise their experience of emotional and/or physical intimacy experiences, either as involved parties, or as third

Case 15   Going Dutch

The 'A'/'B' quote highlighted above, is one of the few examples of an affair at senior management levels which seriously deteriorated the performance of the 'top team' due to the status differences between the two persons. 'A' is a Dutchman, the managing director (MD) responsible for the largest and most profitable division of a large multi-national corporation. 'B' is the female R&D director, sitting on 'A's senior management divisional team. She too is Dutch. A year after being appointed, 'A' recruited 'B'. As 'B' is the only woman on the team, the other team members initially assumed that 'A's concern for 'B' was to positively facilitate her settling into the organisation and, particularly, into the senior management group. However, their friendliness continued. Suspicions became aroused when a high profile project carried by 'B's department began to miss significant cost and revenue targets. At a subsequent meeting, the responsibility for the project was transferred to the Director of Marketing on the pretext that the project in question had progressed beyond research and development and now needed marketing expertise. Despite the opposition from the marketing director, whose view was that the project should be scrapped due to its lack of viability, the programme of activity was transferred to marketing. A year later, the project was over budget and had missed its revenue targets. The marketing director was openly criticised at one of the year end budget review meetings. He was interviewed after the meeting.

Marketing Director: 'I have to tell you, I am seriously contemplating resigning. I have had enough of those two Dutch idiots.'

Interviewer: 'Please explain what's happening.'

Marketing Director: 'When she was first appointed, we thought he was friendly and supportive to help her into the organisation. Not long after, they were seen together having dinner in a manner that was not just one of great colleagues. One of the directors on the senior team knows people in her previous organisation. What do we find out? They have been having an affair for years. Both of them married, and both of them pretending they hardly know each other.'

He paused: 'To be honest, I could not care less what they do. But when her pet IT project, which all our colleagues said was going to fail starts failing and I am given the job of putting the bits together, that's when I get really angry. I am carrying someone else's failures just because the boss is having an affair with her. The team dislike her. She is manipulative. But, they hate him! We've decided we are going to get them both and to be honest with you that is probably the only reason I am still here!'

Male Marketing Director, International IT Communications Company party onlookers, affected or not, 60 per cent of respondents express positive sentiments.

- 'Learning experience.'
- 'Exciting.'
- 'Enhancing.'
- 'Development! It teaches you how to handle people and be more aware.'
- 'Extremely positive, and still growing in our marriage.'

The majority of positive comments refer to learning – learning how to 'work through' uncomfortable and sensitive diversities, or more generally, developing in one's self the qualities to better address the challenges of people management.

Of the fewer negative comments made, the majority refer to managing difficult people issues.

- 'Emotionally draining. I spent a lot of time listening, supporting.'
- 'Emotionally expensive for those involved and for me or the manager who has to deal with this.'
- 'Uncomfortable.'

Equally, certain respondents recognise that they should learn not to repeat the uncomfortable experience of an intimate relationship at work. However, a few indicate that they are still tempted (Case 16).

- 'Never do it again! But, again, if someone gorgeous comes in I would go for it! Crazy! I should have learnt but then look at some of the lovelies that are here!'

The individual in Case 16 was divorced three years later. The ostensible reason was another affair at work but this time, without loss of job. However, more prolonged discussion highlighted that the individual's father behaved much the same. That family's history was riddled with divorce, affairs, and re-marriage. Although the instability in the family was recognised, the desire to confront what seemed to be a pattern of learned behaviour was not forthcoming. As far as the economist was concerned, someone else was to blame. For him, when a personal relationship or job did not proceed satisfactorily, 'never look back; just move on'. It emerged in conversation that that was also the motto of the economist's father. Although few report such extremes of

---

Case 16   *My Problem is Zippergate*

The above comments were made by a male senior professional, an economist, employed by an internationally renowned bank.

Question: You mean you would do the same again?

Answer: Crazy as it may sound but the answer is probably yes. I have been sacked twice before for affairs at work. I have been divorced once before. My present wife is the result of an affair at work. Thankfully, I did not get the sack because of her. I married her.

Question: Why do it?

Answer: Why indeed! Well, I am hard working. I am ambitious. I do want to get on, so most of my time is spent at work. That does not leave much time for anything else. Second, I need to feel close to people at work otherwise the place is boring. I like people, which means I am urged to get to know others, and for me to work well, I need to get to like people. In that sense, I suspect, I am not that unusual. Most people continue working in their place because they get on with people. I suppose the difference between me and them is, I am not as inhibited as them. I express myself that extra step.

Question: You mean to the point of being required to leave twice?

Answer: Well that is unusual I grant you, but you see, as I like people, I like them to like me as well. Having that attention is important and if you think that is unusual just look around here at this place. Very few people can say that they do not desire attention, or if given to them, they feel great. I have to be honest and say that I do not see myself as that unusual, just perhaps unlucky.

Question: You said that your relationship with your wife arose out of an affair at work, how is that progressing?

Answer: Oh fine. We have three children and we are getting on fine. Oh, and before you ask me, this time it is for life. I have something good and I do not wish to spoil it.

Question: But how does that tie up with your original comment that if someone else as lovely came along, you may still be tempted?

Answer: That's true. I suppose I would like to think this is for life but I am still young and ambitious. Perhaps my problem is zippergate. With most people it goes up and stays up. With me it goes up and down. Problem is I like it that way.

Senior Economist and Banker

behaviour, his circumstances of unresolved familial patterns of relationships emerging in the next generation, is highlighted by a minority of respondents in this survey.

IT Revolution

A number of interviewees suggest that advances in IT greatly enables communication through electronic mail, voice mail, internet, and thus facilitates greater intimacy of relationships.

The majority of respondents view electronic media based communication as 'more promoting openness and interest in others' (Table 3.11). One reason offered is that IT is a more 'neutral' channel of communication and, as such, people feel less inhibited to express themselves. Typing messages which appear on a screen is easier than making direct comment face to face. A number of respondents view e-mail as a seductive tool, as messages can be more easily sent whilst ensuring for perceived higher levels of confidentiality. A number report that only the two individuals involved will know of their intimacy interest in each other.

• 'It is easier to get in touch with someone else through e-mail, especially when you want it kept secret.'

The introverted nature of the two individuals in Case 17 and their greater comfort in growing a relationship through IT mediated communication, captures the experiences of a considerable number of the study's respondents. However, similar to so many others' experience, once the relationship became more established, it did not progress to a satisfactory end. The controlled environment of technologically mediated communication is viewed as inappropriate to the 'ups and downs' of real life. However, the outcome of the relationship in Case 17, reaching confrontation and lawyers, is more extreme than most participants report.

Table 3.11 IT Impact on Intimacy Experience

	Total (%)	Male (%)	Female (%)
Promoting	58	32	26
Inhibiting	12	9	3
No impact	30	21	9

Case 17 The Paradox of a Virtual Relationship – Trust or Treachery?

It was early September and I returned from summer vacation to find myself assigned to a new project. Our department had been facilitating the development of an international health services research and training collaboration. An external consultant had been responsible for the file but had encountered some difficulty in moving the project ahead. Our Director asked me to take the file.

Essentially, my role was to work with a European professor to complete the development of the concept, the business plan and funding proposal. This individual had previously visited our organisation and met with a number of local stakeholders but, as I was relatively new to the organisation, I had not met him.

I was to work with him via e-mail to complete a final draft of the work in progress. I knew that English was not his first language and, while I was concerned about how well we might be able to collaborate virtually, my biggest concern was that I had absolutely no background in the health services field. A colleague with the necessary background was assigned to advise me on substantive issues and we began the task at hand. Interactions were sporadic over the first three months. The professor was very prompt in responding to my drafts and offering valuable feedback.

For me, the assignment was both intriguing and a source of stress. I enjoyed the new learning – and the challenge – but found the expectations of local project stakeholders to be very demanding as I juggled this with a number of other assignments. I was determined to put my head down, get the job done and move on.

It's really hard to explain how the virtual relationship between this man and I changed over the coming months but it certainly did. At first, it was simply his offering additional information about his personal and professional activities – never gratuitously but rather as context for why he might have delayed a reply to an e-mail or why I might expect to wait for a reply in the coming days. He was very appreciative of my work and very encouraging and this helped to alleviate some of my anxiety around the assignment – my performance anxiety and fear of failure!

The longer we continued this intermittent virtual correspondence, the more interested I became in knowing more about this person. I didn't want to make my curiosity obvious to others in the organisation but I would ask those who had met him what he was like. The comments back were nothing very exciting other than that he was middle aged, rather reserved and remote and 'not the sort of person you would take note of in an airport lounge ... rather ordinary'. Strangely, this only served to peak my curiosity but I was focused on getting the assignment done and off my desk.

Then, in mid-December, I received a short and cheery message from him – not a reply to an e-mail from me regarding the latest draft – but instead telling me that he was leaving that week to travel to his home for the Christmas vacation, that he would be away until the new year and wished me a very happy Christmas. I was inexplicably touched to receive the e-mail; then found myself wondering where his home was, who was his family, was he married, children ..... . I went home to my own family – a husband and two children – but found myself continuing to think about him throughout the holiday period.

Over the coming months, the frequency of our virtual interactions increased as the project planning progressed. We started to share casual exchanges around the weather, world events and our respective areas of expertise and research. Gradually, he began to take me into his confidence regarding concerns he had related to the work we were doing together and especially with regard to individuals that he had previously worked with and found difficult or not to be trusted.

He then sent along a notice for a special seminar that he was giving at his university and suggested that I should come. I was thrilled but really couldn't justify the expense given that I saw my involvement with the project winding down as the development work was nearing completion. Even though I really didn't want to end this virtual friendship, I didn't expect it to continue once the funding was secured and the project was ready for start-up. When I expressed this to him, he wrote back very quickly sharing an amended business plan that included a revised position description for the project manager. The new description stated clearly that the individual would be appointed by him and required the very qualifications that I possessed. Well.... I was flattered and I was hooked.

It suited my organisation to accept his wishes on this matter. Frankly, most people who had already worked with him were baffled as to how well we were working together and how I seemed to have been able to move him along in accepting some of the parameters that other stakeholders were insisting be part of the proposed collaboration. My ability to keep him 'on side' and keep the project moving forward had earned me a great deal of recognition within the organisation. This continued to be a challenge over the coming months as we moved to final funding approval but I worked very hard to keep the project on target.

We e-mailed each other several times each day and gradually, I found myself more and more aligned with his position and working to deliver the project to him as he envisioned it. The local stakeholders were prepared to let him have his way for the most part and we finally signed off on the deal in mid-May. He then suggested that it was time for me to visit him so that we could continue planning for the project start-up.

I was anxious to meet him after several months of virtual collaboration but I was also apprehensive. What if, after all of these months of working together virtually, we didn't hit it off face to face? Still, I couldn't resist the chance to finally meet him and see whether my projections – and my fantasies – about him were at all realistic. By this time, I had tracked down a video-taped lecture that he had delivered and we had participated in one teleconference along with my Director and another colleague. So, I knew what he looked like and had heard his voice.

Three weeks later, I was waiting in my hotel room for him to call for me and take me to his office. It felt very awkward to finally meet. We were both introverted by nature and had become accustomed to the controlled environment of e-mail interaction. However, within a few minutes we were sharing a laugh. His colleagues were very friendly and welcoming but obviously surprised and curious about the casual and comfortable way in which we interacted as this was not the norm in their work environment. His two closest colleagues – both women – had worked with him for more than ten years and did not enjoy this easy rapport with him.

I was certainly flattered and began to feel that we did have a special relationship. I found myself thinking about the possibility of an affair with him. Did I want this? Yes, I did but I also recognised what was at risk for me both personally and professionally. I wondered if I could settle for a good friendship – a close but not an intimate relationship. I decided that this would be the best all around but I wasn't entirely convinced that it was really what I wanted.

We enjoyed three days of meeting and working face-to-face plus sight seeing, dinners and a rock concert. The concert was my suggestion and totally out of character for him as was obvious from the reaction of his colleagues. Everything was very proper. No personal or sexual advances were made. I did notice that he was very careful about who I met and how much information they were given about who I was and why I was visiting. I found it a bit odd at the time but trusted him so completely that it never crossed my mind to consider why. I just attributed this to his rather reserved and careful nature.

Over the summer months, we continued to put plans in place for the start-up of the project. He then visited our organisation in late summer. We had a very busy week with many meetings. I found him becoming rather distracted as the week progressed. I attributed this to jet lag and to his being anxious about ensuring a successful project launch. I sensed that there was something amiss but I couldn't put a finger on it. In retrospect, I think that deep down I was beginning to recognise that the fantasy of a special relationship with this man was just that – a fantasy that would not be sustained.

The wheels really came off the wagon – so to speak – over the following weeks as we found ourselves grappling with the pressures of start-up details and deadlines. We had been preoccupied with concerns about the reliability of the videoconference technology that we were planning to use as our main operational medium. Ironically, the technology posed no problems but the cultural and interpersonal dynamics of virtual organisation were to be our Achilles heel.

At the very time that we needed to be in close communication, I found him distancing himself. He no longer responded promptly to e-mails as he had in the past. Phone messages were not returned. I was frustrated and confused. I felt like I had been abandoned to sort out the problems on my own.

At the same time, he was becoming very controlling. He began to use his two close colleagues as an interface between he and I. He insisted that he was the one to make final decisions on all aspects of project operations while at the same time not responding to questions and concerns. When of necessity I moved to resolve issues on my own, he was extremely annoyed and suggested that my role would need to be redefined. I was devastated and could not understand what had happened.

Our ability to work together continued to deteriorate and eventually I had to advise the local stakeholders that I could not continue to work with him nor could I recommend the project continue to be funded. There were several unresolved issues pertaining to the project. Further, the potential for legal liability around these matters was to be vested with the local stakeholders. Putting this matter on the table is one of the most difficult things I have ever had to do. Professionally, I knew that I had to do it but personally, I was delivering the final blow to what had been such a magical relationship.

With the support of the local stakeholders, I was entrusted to work with our lawyers to wind up the project and sever our ties with this man. It was heart breaking. The whole process took several months. Throughout the process, I had to keep my feelings in check and maintain my professionalism. Inside, I was dying.

I continued to puzzle over what had happened and why everything had changed so dramatically. This is certainly one of the drawbacks to virtual collaboration. There are so many gaps in information, context and understanding that it is almost impossible to make sense in such a situation especially when the other party has withdrawn and will not offer any type of explanation. This was very hard for me to accept as I need closure and could not get it. Nothing made sense. Sorting fantasy from reality became impossible.

A close colleague suggested that, given what had transpired, this man did not appear to have been trustworthy and may have intentionally manipulated my feelings to gain my trust and convince me to stay the course getting the project in place according to his wishes. I still find it hard to accept this partly because I am embarrassed to think that I was used in this way and partly because – even seven years later – I still do not want to believe that he would have intentionally acted in this way.

Personal learning ...

I've come to recognise that perhaps I was as attracted to the challenge of achieving a close relationship with this man. I am a very competitive person when it comes to a challenge. I like to achieve. I think when I discovered that others had tried and failed to get him on side in this collaborative venture, I was determined to succeed. Perhaps I just got carried away. As a result, I've learned to keep a healthy distance between personal and professional affairs regardless of the temptation or the challenge on offer.

And as difficult as it was, I did learn that I could do what was necessary when I had to – that I could maintain my professionalism. I also learned to trust my inner voice – the one that was telling me early on that all was not as I might wish it to be. My trust meter is much more sensitive today and I do take it into account when I am meeting and dealing with new associates and clients.

Ironically, this experience has actually served as a major impetus for my career progression. Despite the ups and downs, through this experience I came to realise how much I love the world of academic research. Three years ago, I enrolled as a part-time PhD student. I hope to complete my degree over the next two years and begin a new career.

Female Ex Project Manager, British Consulting Organisation

Others in the study consider IT as a negative mode of communication and highlight the increased possibility of sexual harassment. Being 'bombarded' with e-mails and voice mails, in effect, no face to face interaction, is reported as an equally harassing experience as personal confrontation. In contrast to direct harassment, some cite the emergence of electronic communication as a positive development in that IT based messages provide evidence and can be used as examples of harassment. Equally, electronic evidence is viewed as having its downsides as certain respondents state they have experienced, or witnessed, an insensitive or unscrupulous individual circulating someone's message of interest or affection to all in the organisation, at the touch of a button. The potential for abuse through electronic communication applies as much to the receiver of, as to the sender of, messages.

Similar to Case 18, one characteristic common to those who report some form of harassment experience through e-mail is either a reluctance or inability to conduct face to face conversation. A supposed inability for intimate conversation is counterbalanced by considerably intimate or even assertive/aggressive comment transmitted electronically. As portrayed by 'A' in Case 18, colleagues find it difficult to believe that someone as 'shy' or non-confrontational could be so bullish through their computer. Further, female harassment of males (through IT based communication or not) is reported in this survey as on the increase, and most of the respondents do not consider that as unusual. What is unusual is that A in Case 18 seemed a most unlikely initiator of harassment. The results of this survey do indicate that some of the most unexpected people harass others.

Management intervention

The survey results highlight two contrasting intervention patterns from management, first towards physical intimacy and separately towards emotional intimacy (Fig. 3.11). Where incidences of physical intimacy, or combined physical and emotional intimacy occur, (i.e., colleagues working together, have an affair and still work together), management's most common reaction is identified as deciding to ignore. Equally, those being managed respond in a similar manner.

- 'Everybody is doing it. Nobody is talking about it.'
- 'Tolerated it. It was a very discrete relationship.'
- 'Tolerant to a point. Tolerant at the surface. We have different standards for males and females.'

Case 18   Too Shy to Speak

I was attached to the strategic planning department at a major international corporation in the UK. There was a research community that existed and I knew of the particular individual concerned, 'A', as she had worked at the organisation for some time.

I met a male colleague of hers 'B' – he shared an office with 'A' – and we had a chat. He thought that it would be useful for all three of us to meet up at some point and talk about the issues concerned with a future possible acquisition.

In due course, we all met up in the office that they both shared and I showed them the kind of things they should be considering when undertaking the planning of a future merger. I thought it was a good meeting and beneficial to all concerned.

A couple of weeks went by and then I received an unusual e-mail. It was a questionnaire that had been designed by 'A'. Not your usual questionnaire but one that asked three questions, along the following lines,

- Do you like going to the cinema?
- Do you like pasta?
- Do you like chocolate cake?

I thought it was an unusual approach. On the one hand I thought it was quite amusing, but on the other, I was slightly concerned by this, not because I could not choose between the three, but because I sensed that 'A' was perhaps developing an interest in me and that I was not in her (and I didn't want to as she was not my type). A few days passed and I thought I would reply, not by filling in the 'questionnaire' but stating that I do like all three but we can share 'as friends'. In retrospect I think this was a mistake and I should have ignored the 'questionnaire', or confronted the situation there and then.

Weeks went by and we did go to the cinema and she cooked me pasta at her place. We also had lunch together once. However, I initially made it clear that I am quite happy to do this, but 'as friends', and I thought she was okay with this. I had a few female colleagues and enjoyed female company, but nothing went on between us, so I thought such an arrangement would be fine.

'A' was a very shy person and it was difficult for her to communicate. Hence, whilst in the work place she used to send me e-mails and the odd card, and on one occasion a bag of chocolates. Yet she never lifted up the phone. On the one hand, I was quite flattered. On the other, I was very concerned, and was not quite sure what to do, or how to stop the situation as I had not been in this position before. I showed these e-mails/cards to someone I knew and obtained her advice. Strangely enough, she was a handwriting expert and the signs were not good – emotional disturbance was one conclusion based on the varying slants of the writing.

On another occasion, 'A' and myself were going to go to an open day and visit a factory that manufactured sports cars. I thought it would be nice to invite a few other friends along to enjoy the experience also. 'A' was not happy with this, so she ended up not coming along, but the rest of us went.

Time went by and the odd e-mail came my way. I chose to ignore them. 'A' was an expert in personality type questionnaires and she knew my 'type'. Based on this, I think she was perhaps expecting me to behave/ respond in a particular way – what it was I don't know, and obviously I wasn't meeting expectations. In retrospect ignoring the e-mails was perhaps not the best thing to do, as I think she was becoming more angry/bitter, and certainly the tones of her e-mails indicated this. This was an added worry for me at the time, as I had just seen a film called Fatal Attraction – the one where the woman ends up boiling his pet rabbit – not that I had a rabbit, but I thought anything unpredictable could happen. I did not know what 'A' was capable of and I guess it caused me some distress at that point.

It all came to a head some months after the initial meeting with 'A' and 'B'. It is difficult to recall the feelings at the time, except that it was becoming distressing and I thought that 'A' and her colleagues in her department hated me (which turned out not to be true).

Anyhow, 'B' was going to leave the organisation and 'A' sent an e-mail asking me if I wanted to attend his 'leaving do'. In it she used phrases like, 'you should not feel obliged to come along', 'you don't have to treat it like some form of emotional obstacle course in order to avoid speaking to me'. I would have gone along anyway, but something inside me became very angry and I picked up the phone to speak to her. She had apparently just left to go home. So I went to the car park to see if I could find her. I took the e-mail and found her. I ended up shouting at her and asking her what the meaning of all of this was and I said that it had to stop. I'm not sure if anyone else saw or heard but I think she was quite embarrassed and agreed not to pursue it any further.

On the next day, I felt I had to speak to 'B' to seek his advice and help to sort it all out. I showed him the e-mail and he was quite shocked. The fact that it was on the organisation's headed paper meant that he thought I had a good case for harassment. I did not want to go down this route. 'B' decided to speak to 'A'. He then spoke to me and said that everything was now okay. Sure enough, time went by and no more e-mails came my way.

Learning points

It was not a pleasant experience at the time – and I guess, there are some messages or learning points,

- I guess male/female friendships are unusual for some people and they may therefore think of it more as a relationship. So perhaps I should not have encouraged friendship outside the work place from the start. I knew she was shy and perhaps she had not been in many relationships, so I should have picked this up sooner.
- I should have confronted issues as they arose, not necessarily because of how they affected me, but because of how they affected her. It should never have got to the stage that it did.

- It has made me think about developing friendships with the opposite sex in the future, and perhaps gauge the situation first, before becoming too friendly, or be perceived as 'leading people on', which was not my intention.
- I am not sure what the learning lessons for 'A' have been. Except that I know that she is now married to someone who is a lot older than she is.

Male Corporate Planner, Multinational Company

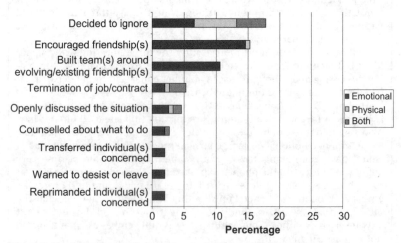

Figure 3.11   Management's Reaction to Intimacy Relationships

- 'Overall, the management style is invisible, off hand. Mind you, the same is for other sensitive issues.'
- 'Practical tolerance, that is the personal style of the leader at the top.'

The practice of tolerance, or turning a 'blind eye', depends partly on the values and style of the manager involved and/or on the degree of anticipated disruption emanating from confronting the parties involved in the intimacy relationship(s). The more discrete the relationship and the less it is perceived as disruptive, the more likely management is to ignore the affair, irrespective of the style of the line manager required to 'deal with the issue'. The more open and unobtrusive the relationship, the less disruptive it is to others, and the more 'tolerant' are the shared attitudes and values in the department/organisation, the more likely managers are to turn 'a blind eye'.

- 'Tolerated, laissez-faire. No big deal.'

- 'Tolerant. Our organisation deals with it more sensitively than is the norm.'
- 'The problem with him [the manager] is that he can handle some people and push them around, but with the one's he cannot, he gives way.'

However, when physical intimacy is obtrusive and causing disruption, management's reaction is more likely to be pronounced, despite the reluctance on the part of management to react. When action is taken, in almost equal measure, termination of job contract is reported to occur, or, more open dialogue is encouraged supported by professional counselling. The study respondents present these two contrasting reactions by management as either one or the other. It is equally high-lighted that management are not consistent in their response, on one occasion pursuing contract termination and on the other, support and counselling. Certain managers in Stages 1 and 2 of the survey were named and accused of favouritism, asking people to leave whom they were perceived not to like, whilst providing support for those with whom they had greater rapport. Other managers seen as inconsistent, are perceived as driven by what they feel they can effectively manage on the day. Reprimands, warnings to desist or leave, or transfer of indi-viduals, are identified as the least utilised management responses. Certainly, being sacked is identified as the preferred management response to warnings or other forms of reprimand.

Despite its untidy conclusion, Case 19 supports the findings of the survey that removal from the workplace is a more likely action to be taken by management than warnings or reprimands. As the senior partner explained to his colleagues,

It was difficult to handle. In the first place, by not having sufficient evidence, and talking it through with the guy, in effect adopting a softer touch, things simply got worse. When I had to see him a second time, the situation had already deteriorated badly. Half the women could have walked out and he still would be taking us to court. The only thing I felt I could do was give him his notice, pay him, have him not turn up to work thereby relieving the tension immediately, knowing that we would face legal proceedings, but only from him!

The partner continued,

People say I should have acted at once – but on what? – potentially slanderous comments on the way he looks? When the evidence

Case 19   Too Sensitive to Handle

The headquarters of a large advertising agency with approximately 240 staff, supported by an additional 120 secretarial and administrative group, was over 60 per cent female. Although the greater proportion of the secretaries and administrators were women, still, just under 45 per cent of the professionals were female. The culture was described by many as being collegial, sharing, organisationally flat (i.e., few status differences, where managers equally held their own client portfolio as well as leading their team), creative and generally, 'a fun place to be'. Equally, most described their involvement with the agency as, 'lucky to be working in such a great place'.

A new manager was appointed to take charge of certain critical corporate relationships. The individual was male, black, UK born and bred, with a home counties (posh) accent, energetic, considered highly innovative and came with an impressive track record. The individual's charm and 'sharp mind' won him many friends, particularly amongst his female colleagues.

After a few weeks, the atmosphere in his senior team began to change. Certain of the women shunned attending his meetings and some openly declined any one to one meetings with him. Shortly, rumours began to circulate that this individual was making lewd suggestions to certain of the female staff and that those women who were described as, 'taking his fancy' would receive phone calls asking for a 'date'. The greater majority declined but then reported that they were subjected to being stared at in meetings and as they walked past his office. No suggestion was made, nor was any complaint lodged that the individual concerned had in any way touched or made any physical gesture towards the women.

These rumours caught the attention of some of the male colleagues. Their response was one of complete surprise.

- 'He has not made a pass at you but it is the way he looks that makes you feel uncomfortable. He can't help that.'
- 'Your problem is that he stares. What the hell can we do about that? On this basis, every man here would have their job threatened.'
- 'You want somebody to take action because he asked you out, which you say he did politely, and because you said no, you feel he sometimes stares at you. Are you sure it's not your imagination?'

As can be seen, the manager concerned was held in high esteem by his male colleagues, as much for his professional skills, his capacity to 'handle' difficult clients, and his sociability for 'mixing' with his 'mates'.

The gossip persisted and eventually it came to the attention of the senior partner in charge of that group. The women subjected to 'the staring' urged the senior partner to act. The men could not substantiate the claims of the women, stating that they had not seen him stare at the women and even if they had, what could be done?

- 'He makes money. He gets the job done. Some of this must be jealousy', was the response of one of his male colleagues.

No action was taken. Yet, the gossip persisted and, in fact, became more pronounced. Many of the women were more openly saying that they did not wish to be in the company of this man. He made them distinctly uncomfortable. After a few weeks, two women, separately, but formally, lodged a complaint against the coloured manager. The senior partner discussed the complaint with the two women, hoping to persuade them to retract. As both refused, the senior partner had little choice but to meet with the manager concerned.

The manager expressed surprise on being informed of the complaint, which quickly turned into anger at the way he was 'being singled out' because of his colour! The senior partner tried to persuade the manager that neither colour, or background, had anything to do with the complaints made, but the concern was his behaviour.

- 'What behaviour? What have I done? As far as I understand this, complaints have been made against me because of the way I look – how am I to take that? – that is just pure prejudice.'

The meeting between the senior partner and manager deteriorated with the manager threatening the partner with legal action if such pressure continued. In order to appease the situation, the senior partner transferred the two females who lodged the original complaints to another section of the organisation.

Yet, the rumours persisted and within weeks, three more formal complaints were made. Two of the women told the senior partner that if something were not done they would resign. One even threatened to approach the press with the story of how bad the working environment had become in the agency due to management's inability to confront 'the sexual politics' of the workplace. By now, a few of the men in the agency commented they had had caught the manager concerned 'looking oddly' at certain of the women.

Feeling that he had no option, the senior partner held a further interview with the coloured manager. The partner, now more assertive, strongly indicated that due to the increasing number of complaints, the situation could not be allowed to continue. The 'staring' that made certain of the women uncomfortable, was being taken by the partner as deliberate 'behaviour' due to the fact that those women in whom the manager had shown no interest, had not made a complaint or offered comment that they felt uncomfortable in his presence. Further, the women that did complain were all younger and generally accepted as 'attractive'.

As before, the meeting deteriorated with the manager accusing the partner of engineering constructive dismissal. After further discussion, the partner stated that the situation had reached a point of no return and the manager would now be given sufficient time to find alternative employment elsewhere. The manager was given three months notice (as stated in his contract) but told he was not required to turn up to work for the next twelve weeks. The manager left that day, threatening legal action.

Presently the senior partners of the firm received formal communication from the manager's solicitors. The senior partner in question was called to a meeting with his senior colleagues to, as one senior partner, commented, 'Explain why staring is a sacking offence, particularly when the guy in question is black.'

International Advertising Agency

mounted, I felt I was justified in doing something, but by then the atmosphere at work was so bad, he had to leave! I do not know how I could have handled it better. I hope I never have to face something like this again!

In contrast, substantially different reactions are reported to circumstances of emotional intimacy. Respondents indicate that most managers view emotional intimacy as friendship, in fact, as a positive phenomenon and thus to be encouraged. The survey respondents highlight that encouraging friendships in the workplace and even building teams around existing friendships, are the second most favoured management reaction (Fig. 3.10).

- 'I worked with more commitment, longer hours.'
- 'We both put more into the job. More achievement and higher performance.'
- 'Greater loyalty to the organisation.'
- 'Project gained a great deal. I put more of my time in it than otherwise.'
- 'In the case of married people, with both in the organisation, they work harder.'

As in Case 20, most managers report that they are unable to identify those emotionally intimate relationships that can 'spill over' and become physically intimate. What they see is a 'greater spirit' with people motivated to work harder, longer and more effectively, as much because of the strong bonds of friendship as by tangible rewards. However, the greater majority of colleagues on the same team/unit or in the same department report they can accurately predict when emotional intimacy becomes, or will become, physical. Under such circumstances, most respondents report passive compliance in ensuring discretion is maintained.

- 'The relationship never surfaced to the attention of management – we made sure of that.'

Company Policy

In examining the policy companies adopt towards intimacy, three questions were explored in the survey,

- Does your organisation have a diversity policy in place?

Case 20 April's Tale

Dr April Taylor, clever, attractive, a microbiologist employed by one of the international pharmaceutical companies, began a platonic friendship with a senior marketing manager from another department but within the same company. Their friendship quickly blossomed facilitated by their second-ment to a temporary project examining the brand potential of a new range of fertility drugs.

Question: You seemed to have struck the right chord from almost the beginning?

Answer: You bet. He was wonderful, really bright, talented, handsome but unfortunately married, and unhappily married. Another reason I took to him is that he was not the sort of person to have an affair. The fact that he was not happy with his private life was not the reason we fell in love. We fell in love because we were right for each other. Both of us wanted the relationship.

Question: Did anyone know?

Answer: Some of our colleagues probably guessed but no-one really knew. Not that it would have made any difference. Our work just got better. If management knew we were having an affair, they may not have liked it, but they would have paid us more to continue. Being together we really produced the results.

Question: In what way?

Answer: We were working on these new fertility drugs. The company in particular, but also this generation of fertility drugs, had received bad press. Our job was to re-brand the drugs, particularly targeting the USA, then Europe. We set up the market trials in extra quick time, run the focus groups, tapped into the opinions of the medical fraternity and the media and completed the main survey and the report three months ahead of schedule. All that and half the time we were apart. He had a number of smaller projects to supervise in the US and I had my own clinical trials here in the UK and France. Yet, being with him, talking to him, as much about work as anything, gave us both a buzz – no – too shallow – deep satisfaction. As our relationship improved so too did the work.

Question: What happened?

Answer: We planned to get married. He was preparing for divorce so that we could marry. Neither of us are for affairs. We are both serious people. Then his wife was diagnosed with a serious cancer. For him, it was pure torment, the reason being he could not leave his wife under those circum-stances. He broke the news to me one evening shortly after he returned from one of his trips to the States, saying we could not get married. Despite how much he loved me, he could not leave his wife. Me, I was devastated. It was what he said next that devastated me even more. You see, I would have waited for him and he knew that, so rather than have me pained for years to come, he had already asked for a transfer which was granted.

> He quickly moved to the USA where he is today. I am not too sure where as he has left the company and joined a competitor. I do not know whether his wife is alive or has since died. For myself, I have married, but a day rarely goes by without me thinking of him.
> What a time, I was really in love, and at work at my most productive. Perhaps such a relationship is too intense and cannot last. Yet, when I look back, I think not. Ours was rare. We were right for each other in every way. It is what romantic novels are made of and I had a glimpse of what life could have been like.
>
> Female Senior Microbiologist Research Manager
> International Pharmaceutical Company

- Is diversity practiced and/or respected, irrespective of whether a formal policy exists?
- What should be the response of your organisation to incidences of physical intimacy?

In response to the first question, the majority of respondents either do not know whether a formal diversity policy exists, or feel that even if it did, it would make no difference to the actions and behaviours of individuals (55 per cent; Table 3.12). Twenty seven per cent however, report they are aware of the existence of a diversity policy in contrast to 18 per cent who indicate that no such policy is in place.

In contrast to the findings of the survey, the individual recounting his experiences in Case 21, hints that if company policies had been in place, the intimacy encounters in the workplace may have been less frequent. Certainly, he captures one finding of the survey, in that, intimacy within a team/group context is more likely to arise especially if the prevailing norms encourage such behaviour. He also highlights one other finding, namely, that a workplace related intimacy encounter can continue for many years.

Additionally, irrespective of the existence of any form of implicit or explicit diversity policy, 63 per cent highlight that management do not respect diversity or attempt to adjust their behaviour when faced with a diversity challenge (Question 2).

- 'Diversity of interests are not well tolerated.'
- 'Do not know, but practice is not pro-active in promoting diversity.'
- 'European Equal Opportunities (EEO) policy in place but diversity is not well respected. It is a conformist environment.'

Table 3.12   Existence of Diversity Policy

	Per cent
Yes	27
No	18
Do not know	30 ⎱ 55%
Makes no difference	25 ⎰

Case 21   No Policies To Speak Of

I'm not sure exactly when I first met L, except that it was about 1970!

I was recently divorced and had moved down to London to work for a large multinational organisation as one of a team of instructors who were training engineers, sales people and customer service representatives. We had all worked closely together for a number of years and several of us shared flats near to where we worked. As a result we often met after work and inter-office relationships were frequent. L and I were part of that group, so we saw each other at work and socially. At first we were just friends but there was soon a special closeness that attracted us both emotionally and physically – we even went off to Paris together for a weekend.

Sadly, perhaps because the relationships amongst the group were becoming more and more volatile and complicated, and I hadn't long been divorced, I was still seeing other people. I know now that this hurt L (and me!) terribly, and we drifted apart. I (we?) didn't realise then that we really loved each other. Soon after, both L and I were in new relationships, and once or twice we even went out as a foursome. I rushed into getting married again and it seemed then as though the relationship between L and I was over.

A year or so later, my wife and I moved out of London and I left the company to work for another multinational organisation! Several people from the training team also joined the organisation – including L, who moved into a house in the same road as me. (I never found out how that happened!) We met a few times, and there were always the overwhelming feelings of closeness and attraction to L that set my pulse racing – but, being married, there was also the guilt and fear of those feelings. So I made excuses and once again backed away.

Apart from the odd occasion I didn't see L again for nearly 20 years, by which time I'd moved up to Northamptonshire, we had a daughter, and L had a son. Coincidentally, both our freelance ventures had fallen victim to the recession (and our mismanagement!). I was out of work, depressed and had taken a job north of London with a 75 mile journey each way on the M1 every day. It was close to where L used to live, and we eventually met up again and all the feelings were still there! We talked and laughed and cried a lot and even tried to plan a future together, but even though my marriage was dismal and L was single, the practicalities of families and children made it impossible. I left my job, went freelance again, and stopped going down to see L. There were a couple of times when we tried to set up some work projects together, but once again, it was the wrong time.

Another seven years brings us to the present. L had moved back to Lancashire a few years earlier but we had managed to keep in touch. I am now settled and very happy at the local university, but my wife wants to move away. We haven't been close for a long, long time so we have at last decided to separate to follow our own interests as soon as she has found the house she would like.

I have seen L recently and the love we felt for each other over 30 years ago is as strong as ever! Perhaps, after all this time, there's still a chance for us to be together!

Undoubtedly the nature and dynamics of the group where we first met made it a lot easier and safer for me to form relationships, because at the time I would probably not have had the courage to even speak to L. But also, perhaps casual relationships were so much easier for me to handle emotionally that I didn't recognise (or want to recognise) one that was much deeper. (So much deeper in fact than I could ever have imagined!) Also, L and I both working in another organisation again made it easier for us to meet again – we might never have done so otherwise. Neither of the multinational companies we worked for had any ethical standards or policies regarding relationships, so office affairs were commonplace and often conducted openly. However, I saw this as being rather sleazy and very destructive and didn't want to be seen in the same light (or was I just envious and too guilt-ridden?).

Male Trainer, Manager and now Academic

Most descriptions of lack of diversity refer to the culture of the organisation and/or the particular attitudes of colleagues and managers within a team or department. Specific examples of poor diversity practice more focus on women, rather than race, colour or ethnicity.

- 'Male relationships are more tolerated than female.'
- 'Far fewer women in this organisation.'

Other examples of poor diversity practice focus on the performance of individuals, teams and/or the organisation. The majority of respondents emphasise how striving for high levels of performance restricts broader diversity thinking.

- 'Quite diverse in terms of gender, race and language, but people have to perform to standards and that creates uniformity.'
- 'Who you are and where you came from does not matter as long as you do the job. What we have here is command and control – no individuality.'

- 'This place is not affirmative action. It does not try to promote minorities. It is only concerned with performance.'

The emerging view is that in organisations where task related performance predominates all other concerns, there is little or no attempt made by management to promote positive discrimination in order to achieve a gender/race/disability balance. High performers who promote diversity concerns are tolerated because of their capabilities and drive to achieve results. Their promotion prospects are unlikely to be harmed but the feeling expressed is that another candidate of equal capability, less concerned with diversity issues, is likely to be preferred. The reason for such preference is that the 'low diversity sensitive' individual would not be viewed as a 'trouble maker'. However, those of average performance and ability, but diversity conscious, may find themselves 'side lined' and their career progress frustrated. Respondents found it difficult to determine whether a person is held back due to their 'average' performance or more due to their 'nuisance' value in promoting enhanced diversity practice.

A minority of respondents (37 per cent) view their organisation and management as positively inclined towards diversity practice.

- 'Equal opportunity is well respected – look at those we have hired who are disabled and blind.'
- 'We have a merit principle here and try hard to apply that to those disadvantaged.'
- 'Sexual harassment is simply not tolerated.'
- 'We have recruited white, European and male and we are doing our best to change that by our investment in people and their development.'
- 'The culture of this organisation is diversity. This is a cosmopolitan place, in all senses of the term.'

The most common response to Question 3, exploring the policy of the organisation to incidences of physical intimacy, is to highlight the lack of sexual harassment. Irrespective of the status of the individual, their gender, their views towards intimacy in the workplace, or the discomfort certain individuals may experience due to the intimacy relations of others, the low incidence of sexual harassment is ranked as top of the list (Fig. 3.12). This finding contradicts the conclusions of certain studies identified in the literature overview of Chapter 2 that physical intimacy and sexual harassment are closely linked in practice or in many people's minds!

- 'I know of only one and he was issued with a written warning.'
- 'I think there was one a long time ago.'
- 'Ironically, harassment of a staff member by students.'
- 'Yes, once. A girl accused a male manager of touching her up. On investigation, it looks as if those two had a history. Both were named. Next time they will both leave.'

Thirty one per cent of the sample, declare they have no knowledge of harassment complaints in the organisation. Of the few that reported such knowledge most comment that sexual harassment occurs rarely in their organisation, and even then, only isolated incidents are identified by the survey respondents. Boss/subordinate harassment is mentioned, but so to is colleague/colleague, male on female as well as female on male, and lecturer on student as well as student on lecturer. The majority of the comments highlight the idiosyncratic nature of each circumstance, namely, as relatively unique to the situation or the personalities involved. Although the majority of the harassment circumstances are reported as 'tackled' by management, most of the respondents comment that similar circumstances are unlikely to re-occur irrespective of the actions of management. Only two per cent of comments refer to a 'cover up', whilst seven per cent of respondents declare themselves as 'too anxious' to raise the issue for fear of repercussion on them, by being seen as 'whistle blowers' by management, or by being the 'target' from the parties involved in the sexual harassment incidence.

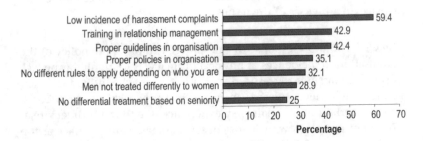

Figure 3.12 Policy Recommendations Towards Physical Intimacy

In keeping with the findings of the survey, the 'unique' nature of the circumstances outlined in Case 22, the stated borderline acceptable/unacceptable behaviour between the woman and her boss, and the fact that her father was the boss's boss, places harassment in the grey zone. The decision made was to be diplomatic rather than lodge a formal grievance. Despite her discomfort, she draws sharp distinction between harassment and emotional encounters that border on undesired physical attention but which do not engender sufficient urgency to take formal action.

Unlike the circumstances outlined in Case 22, the female project manager of Case 23 presents less of a blurring between intimacy and harassment. On her admission she still made no formal complaint. The experience however, has left her fragile. The question remains as to whether the low reported incidence of harassment accurately reflects its low incidence or whether the fear factor of harassment inhibits individuals from even raising the topic.

Yet, irrespective of the experiences captured in Case 23, the survey respondents do go to considerable lengths to draw sharp distinction between harassment and physical intimacy (as in Case 22). A number of the respondents point out that physical intimacy can leave either party vulnerable to a harassment complaint but that is not harassment of a sexual nature. Some of the harassment incidents reported are viewed as unjustifiably made. It is considered that in the majority of known harassment cases, the parties involved had entered into the relationship willingly, with no evidence of undue pressure made on one person by the other at that point.

Whether for reasons of harassment or not, most of the survey respondents concur that formal intervention is required if unfair treatment of an individual occurs, or, if individual, team and organisational performance is damaged. Despite the need for clear intervention, three areas of concern surface concerning the organisation's response to intimacy, namely that,

- certain individuals are 'protected', or treated more harshly because of who they are
- different attention is afforded to men as opposed to women
- those of higher seniority are treated with greater or lesser leniency

Effective policy and guideline application is considered to be particularly dependent on the skills and sensitivity of senior management and the overall equity orientation of the organisation. Management that

Case 22   *The Grey Area of Office Behaviour: A Canadian Perspective*

Once, during a rough search for employment, my friend Matt bitterly stated, 'It's so much easier being a good looking girl. You get a job just like that.' Now a few years later, and a member of Vancouver's business community, I reflect on his statement with some annoyance. His statement is both true and ignorant at the same time ...

I do agree that being attractive does help anyone get attention, including prospective employers. However, being a female that falls under Matt's description, I can confirm that there are certainly disadvantages. Consider a recent situation.

I adore my boss and believe that he is truly a very genuine man. He is a hard worker and caring about everything he does. I have worked for him for about three years and have developed a close relationship with him. Close ... in the sense that I view him as a father figure. It is also important to mention that his boss IS my father. During my three years at the company I was able to grow and take on more and more responsibilities. My boss always encouraged this, and often expressed how bright he thought I was. However, slowly as time progressed, I began to notice behaviour that was a little less fatherly ... though at the same time not offensive. I believe that this is not an uncommon situation for anyone.

It appears that with so many social pressures exerted on a work environment, including the notion that one's job is at stake, unacceptable behaviour is more difficult to define. Consider this example. A stranger in a park makes the following comment to a woman passing by, 'You are so beautiful and bright', and then puts his arm around her. Immediately, the woman would process the situation as offensive or flattering in an amorous way. If the same comment was made to a woman from her boss or colleague, she may not necessarily find it offensive but would likely think about the comment before deciding how she feels about it, i.e., 'It's my boss, he's just being complimentary. He isn't jeopardising our working relationship or his position?' or, 'Hmmm, I suppose that was nice, though I'm not quite sure where his intentions lie.'

It wasn't until repeated incidences of this type of behaviour, that I began to question my boss's motives. In addition to analysing the comments, I was very hesitant to make any final decisions about how they affected me.

Upon realising that this behaviour truly did make me feel uncomfortable, I became overly aware of all of his actions, including behavioural tendencies that have never bothered me in the past. This over-awareness caused me considerable distress and disappointment. I really respected the man and had adored working under him. After an extensive period of analysis, I concluded that I was in quite a dilemma.

Firstly, my boss's actions were not exactly incriminating. His actions included touching my shoulders, putting his arms around my waist, and tapping my thighs. Therefore, I didn't really feel strongly enough to bring the issue up with him or anyone else. I concluded that discussing the situation with him in a frank, polite and discreet manner would still make him feel uncomfortable and could potentially mar our working relationship forever. Taking the issue up with somebody else would destroy his reputation and working relationships with every colleague at the office. So, despite the uncomfortable feelings I experienced, I felt that it was wise to keep these sentiments to myself.

Today, I still believe that this was the right decision. I continue to work for my boss and am happier about the situation. Now that I am aware of his behaviour and my feelings about it, I am better able to ignore or prevent opportunities for this behaviour to trigger. While it seems like a lot to think about, I firmly believe that my resolve to keep 'things quiet' was the right choice.

I suppose most women, feminist or not, reading this short case would likely cry 'bloody murder'. How could I turn my back on such behaviour? Simple. Things like this happen and the smartest move in such situations is to internalise and respond productively. This is what I did.

I firmly believe that there are sometimes situations that arise where WE the women (or male *vice versa*) have to be the stronger actors. A case in point response to Matt's ignorant statement, 'Good looking girls don't exactly get it easy.'

Lastly, it is important to understand that while I view my experience as bordering on acceptable, in no way do I condone sexual harassment or assault at the office. MY story is meant to only enlighten those that see office harassment as a black and white situation. More often than not there is a grey area ... a continuum of unacceptable to acceptable behaviour.

Female Manager, Mid Sized Canadian Company

attempts to appropriately model the required employee behaviour is more likely to be respected by the staff of the organisation. In contrast, whatever policies and guidelines are in place, they are seen as meaningless if the leaders of the organisation do not exemplify the attitudes, values, desired behaviours, or, do not attempt to cultivate open dialogue (see Case 24).

As highlighted in the introduction, the terms rational and limbic do hold particular meaning concerning the conduct of personal relationships. Understanding towards one's own predicaments and emotional challenges but rationally disciplined towards others, virtually ensures that respect ceases. Fear became the only 'motivator' the Chairman/CEO (Case 24) could ultimately exercise. Even his own team learnt

Case 23   *From Special Friendship to Harassment*

Unfortunately my story is similar to many.

It all started because I had been assigned to a project where Jim was working as well. He was a kind person – so I thought at first – full of life and fun to be with. I had been warned that people who worked for him feared him, but I didn't believe that. I thought these were rumours spread by envious people.

Our project required us to have meetings on a very regular basis. We enjoyed each other's company and we used to socialise with other colleagues outside work. I thought Jim liked me and I thought our 'friendship' was special.

A year went by and then another and then ... the unexpected. I started to feel uneasy because it seemed as if he wanted to control me, he wanted to control my life and was starting to treat me as if I was his wife. He expected me to receive his phone calls at any time of the day and would get really upset if I had to stop the conversation. I felt as if I was pushed to phone him back when I didn't want to.

Then the e-mails. We had exchanged e-mails in the past but now it had become a chore. I was blamed for not responding or for the length of the response, the lack of exclamation marks, etc ...

Everything started to become unnatural and I started to withdraw. The more trapped I felt, the more Jim would phone and repeat endlessly that I was betraying our friendship and I was really selfish.

I had become a sort of obsession for him. He admitted he would think of me every day, before he went to bed, when he woke up and he was compelled to get in touch with me by any means. He would get very upset if I wasn't prepared to stay on the phone for long. I was charged with high treason for destroying such a beautiful 'friendship'.

I started not to answer the phone because the calls started to be really unbearable. I was the reason for all this unhappiness, I was the source for all this sorrow. If only I responded, if only I put more effort into building this friendship, we could be very happy. I didn't think this was the truth.

Endless calls, a myriad of text messages. I had voice mail and, of course, he started to leave messages, one nice, one nasty, one nasty, one nice. I could receive six or seven messages all three or four minutes long. I was scared. I could not answer my mobile or even my home number without fear. I would get agitated whenever somebody rang.

But I persisted. I never answered any of my mail, never returned any call, asked to be moved to a different project and made my position very clear to him. I think he hates me and despises me for this but I didn't have any choice. I was going mad and I could not carry on like this.

I still feel some regrets about this. Unfortunately this horrible story has changed my approach to people. I used to send mail with jokes and funny remarks, exclamation marks, etc. Now, I am very matter of fact. I really don't like it and I have to force myself to behave this way. I have no choice. I can't re-live the nightmare that caused me so much pain.

Female Project Manager, Large Multinational

Case 24   Rational About You Lot; Limbic About Myself

The Chairman/CEO of a major US multinational (the individual held both roles), supposedly happily married to his dentist wife, surprised everyone in the organisation by leaving his wife and entering into an intimate relationship with his secretary. Seen by his colleagues and subordinates as an unfeeling, stern, totally corporately minded and profit driven senior executive, his attitude seemingly changed with the restructuring of his personal circumstances. Since the break up with his wife, he was described as more understanding of others, particularly those who experienced emotional and personal disruption. He was seen as a much nicer guy!

However, this new found warmth was not to last. Divorced from his first wife, he married his secretary shortly after.

'That's when things went back to normal,' said his senior executives.

'The same old fellah came back. Intolerant of others, straight laced, everything was success, profits and the organisation. Certainly completely intolerant of people's private problems and extra marital relationships, when he was the one who publicly went through a work related sexual encounter,' continued the senior manager.

'Well, I can tell you. Anything to do with my emotions and me has just gone underground. People are more defensive now than before. If anything, things are worse and respect for the Chairman is virtually zero, but no one will tell him. I have been doing this part time psychology course at the local university. In learning about human psychology, I was introduced to the terms rational and limbic. Well, I can tell you, the worst thing to do as a top manager is be rational towards everybody else and limbically understanding towards oneself. We can't wait for that shit to leave.'

Male British Subsidiary CEO discussing his Chairman/Group CEO
US International Commodity Company

---

how to skirt around him. In contrast to the corporate culture of most US corporations, where loyalty to the top man (or woman) is paramount, a number of managers gleefully celebrated his departure from the organisation.

Additionally, more entrepreneurial organisations composed of independently minded individuals, where success is contingent on the individual's self determination, are identified as inappropriate contexts for policy and rule application.

- 'Policies would not work in this individualistic place.'
- 'Inappropriate here where people are so creative.'

In entrepreneurially oriented environments, the expectation is that staff and middle management would collude to undermine formal policies because of their shared antipathy to the constraining effect of procedure and regulation. The existence of formal guidelines and rules are seen as inhibiting individual and group effectiveness as the market requires people to be flexible and undaunted by internal procedures.

4
Addressing Intimacy

The majority of respondents in this survey report experiencing intimate relationships within the workplace. Further, the critical conclusion to emerge from this survey is that people enter into intimate relationships within the work context because they want to! Of those that enter into physical intimacy, most are 'boy meets girl' stories, with both parties single and, for the majority, both parties making sure that their work effort and output are not compromised.

In fact, most report positive benefit from the experience and in cases of emotional intimacy, a considerable proportion of survey respondents emphasise the supportive response from their employing organisation. When closer and more positive relationships are formed, people report that they work better together, work harder to achieve their objectives and through such mutual respect and care, the organisation is also viewed in a more positive light. Equally, a substantial proportion of the survey respondents view physical intimacy in a positive light, either as parties directly involved or as third party onlookers. Overall, it is reported that work effectiveness increases as a result of the relationship.

The survey results also show that managers may not ever be aware of most physically intimate relationships that occur. However, managers do recognise that emotional intimacy can easily migrate to physical intimacy. Despite such insights, emotional intimacy is encouraged.

Additionally, a number of respondents support the emerging conclusions of other studies discussed in Chapter 2, that the distinction between home and work life is becoming blurred. One respondent described his office as,

- '... the table or desk where I position my computer to do my work is my office. It could be a desk at the workplace or the bedside table next to my bed.'

Accompanying the blurring of home and work life are comments concerning fatigue. The 'working longer' characteristic emerges in this study as in so many others identified in Chapter 2. As the workplace becomes more concerned with social affiliation, so too is it a drain on people's lives. Working harder and longer results in people being tired. Thus, though incidences of physical intimacy occur more frequently, the level of fatigue to do little more than sleep once at home is also on the rise.

Just like so many politicians, business people, clergy and members of the armed forces, discussed in Chapter 2, this survey on workplace intimacy reports similar experiences for basically 'every day folk'! Not that our notable public figures offer a poor example. Our survey respondents indicate they pursue their desires and instincts irrespective of what our public leaders do or do not do. In fact, many survey respondents display considerable irritation with the Christian 'right or wrong' moral perspective on intimacy. If anything, the attitudes highlighted in the survey lean more towards a mixture of Judaism, Buddhism and the more liberal end of Hinduism. As the ancient and medieval orders of a distant past instituted punishment for so called 'moral sexual wrong doing', which seemingly did not prevent sexual activity outside the home, so today, the frustration with not taking a broader view emerges as a significant finding.

Nor is it reported that our social fabric is disintegrating. The journey into the history of intimacy pursued in Chapter 2, strongly suggests that considerable sexual activity outside marriage or the home has occurred at different points in time and which, in turn, had little impact on the social engineering of the day. The same finding emerges from this survey.

The various types of relationship and motives identified in the literature (Pierce *et al*, 1996; Powell and Foley, 1998; Lobel *et al*, 1994; Mainiero, 1986; Quinn, 1977), which range from liking, different forms of love and no love, are equally reported by the survey respondents. Some of the survey participants state they just 'liked' their partners and still entered into a sexual liaison whilst others fell deeply in love but did not sexually proceed any further. Despite the level of emotional involvement and the motivation of the parties involved, still the majority of intimate encounters do not emerge as problematic to the individuals concerned, to third parties or to the overall organisation (Markiewicz *et al*, 2000). Thus, the question remains – just what needs to be done with intimate occurrences at work? Are the two common reactions by management, do nothing or loss of employment, sufficient? How should intimate occurrence(s) in the workplace be considered? Just what is the problem? – are intimate relationships in the workplace so abnormal?

The survey respondents were asked, from their experience as third party observers, or from direct involvement in an intimacy relationship at work, what alternative effective ways could be adopted to addressing intimacy encounters? Further, what advice would they give to individuals involved in, or embarking on, intimacy within the workplace?

The greater proportion of responses indicate that no generic prescription concerning appropriate action can be identified (Table 4.1). Each case has to be judged on its merits. Rather than rigidly following organisational policies, the sensitivity and skill of each manager to facilitate a way through emotionally complex situations is emphasised. On the basis that people are increasingly spending more time at work, a considerable number of respondents consider it normal that the incidence of intimacy inclined relationships will rise, irrespective of whether they are, or are not, sexually consummated. Therefore, in order to effectively deal with intimacy, the challenge in the eyes of the respondents is to determine just what is the problem at hand. The occurrence of intimacy, of itself, is not viewed as a concern. The disturbance of third party relationships in the workplace and deterioration of performance, or harassment, are considered as appropriate reasons for management to intervene.

Table 4.1   Approaches to Addressing Intimacy Encounters

	Per cent
Case by case	36
Greater tolerance	24
Management intervention	16
Non interference	13
Well handled	11

In fact, numerous respondents report that, on reflection, what may have been viewed as a problem was given unwarranted, undue attention and that in itself is the prime cause for concern.

- 'Why should management react badly to an office romance?'
- 'Why can we not be seen together at the office party? – more time is lost pretending.'

Hence, 24 per cent of respondents recommend that management be more tolerant of cases of intimacy. In the opinion of most, irrespective of the attitudes and reactions of management, intimacy in the workplace will occur and continue to occur. Nurturing a climate of greater openness is more likely to attract a more mature response from those directly involved and affected third parties.

As part of nurturing a more diversity conscious environment in the organisation, the survey respondents make two recommendations; provide training in relationship management and institute appropriate guidelines on how to address intimacy occurrences. Irrespective of gender, position or job role, 'appropriate' training is viewed from the perspective of 'acceptable' behaviour. However, what is acceptable will vary in each separate workplace. Approaches to training, encompass issues such as managing relationships, understanding the phenomenon of diversity, developing communication and counselling skills, encouraging awareness of the 'mid life crisis' experience, promoting team building and effective team work, providing support and projecting appropriate role models for young and inexperienced people. Interestingly, the survey participants could not clearly identify just what is acceptable workplace behaviour but more what it is not! Respondents comment,

- 'What we need here is more training in life skills and what people need to do to respect differences.'
- 'We need to consider our image internally and externally and believe our image in our day to day affairs. If we do not, we will lose credibility with our clients and the press.'
- 'We are a service organisation. We have a reputation to maintain. Of course affairs will occur from time to time. It is how we handle them that will keep our reputation intact!'

Addressing intimacy concerns involves being conscious of, or at least knowing, how to react when exposed to the press or media. Some of the respondents offered comment on how to coach people to better handle intimacy encounters, others focused on image and managing the expectations of others.

- 'Do what you like as long as it looks OK to the outside world.'

In contrast, a minority of survey respondents consider training on how to address physical intimacy, as inappropriate.

- 'Too paternalistic.'
- 'Too costly.'
- 'People learn and develop through experience.'
- 'If people fall in love. No training will stop that.'

A similar view is adopted concerning the introduction of guidelines and policies in the organisation. The request from the respondents is for guidance, not prescription, particularly in relation to,

- strengthening the integrity of professional relationships,
- the unbiased recruitment, selection, appraisal and promotion of individuals,
- the declaring of a conflict of interests arising from holding any managerial or supervisory responsibility and a personal relationship be it a family or sexual/romantic one,
- ensuring that no prejudicial outcome will arise from declaring any conflict of interests,
- providing a confidential facility in the organisation where guidance on conflicts of interest can be provided,
- providing support and 'protection' for those compromised and in a subordinate role,
- ensuring that pressure is not brought to bear to terminate the relationship if the individuals concerned have appropriately adhered to the guidelines on conflict of interest, and
- confidentiality being maintained at all costs.

Despite such recommendations, a considerable proportion of respondents expressed scepticism to the introduction of policies that would ultimately regulate the incidence of intimacy in the workplace.

- 'Policies impinge on individual freedom.'
- 'Passion cannot be stopped through guidelines.'

- 'One can never outlaw intimacy because that would mean leaving your emotions at the front door of your home!'

Other than obvious disruption to others, harassment or damage to performance, no particular pattern emerges concerning the reasons for management to intervene in an intimacy situation. Certain respondents are driven by their personal view concerning whether intimacy should, or should not, be tolerated in the workplace. Others perceive a prejudicial reaction by management. In complete contrast, others view management as too passive, allowing situations to deteriorate. Certainly, the wide spectrum of reasons offered for greater or lesser management involvement adds to the case by case view promoted by the majority. Only 11 per cent of respondents consider that the cases in which they had direct or indirect involvement were handled well by management.

At a more personal level, a substantial number of respondents, with direct or indirect experience of intimacy, state that they have, or if required, would give advice to others on matters of intimacy in the workplace (Table 4.2). Fifty two per cent, of respondents highlight that the nature of their comments/advice relates to assisting the parties concerned to take a realistic stock of their circumstances. Being realistic requires taking into account the 'attitude of management and colleagues', the level of gossip in the team or department, the maturity of colleagues and management to react appropriately and the overall attitudes and culture(s) prevalent in the organisation. The aim in giving advice is for neither party to be damaged personally, job and/or career wise, but for them to be enabled to 'better handle' their situation. In contrast, 19 per cent of respondents state that they would offer a more judgemental perspective, advising others not to enter into an intimacy relationship. The reasons given are the potential damage to personal, departmental or even organisational reputation, damage to career

Table 4.2   Advice on Intimacy

	Per cent
Be realistic	52
Do not do it	19
Be discrete	12
Be open	9
No advice	6
Introduce formal policy	2

prospects and to already established personal relationships should the intimacy encounter become public.

The contrary view to 'not to do it', is for 12 per cent of the survey participants to state, 'OK, go ahead but be careful!' On the basis that intimacy in the workplace will continue to occur, offering the advice of 'be discrete' is tantamount to tacit permission to go ahead. Others state (nine per cent; Table 4.2) that they would offer the advice of, be open and do little to hide what, in their view, is a natural phenomenon. Still others suggest constraint if either or both parties are married, but for unattached people, 'go for it'!

A further six per cent of respondents indicate that they would not offer advice. The reason given is that mature adults should decide for themselves the quality of life they desire to lead without interference from others. Only two per cent recommend adopting formal policies and guidelines as the means of minimising the incidence of 'office romances' or any undesired outcomes from work related intimacy. As highlighted, the greater proportion of respondents do not support policy based intervention. Most feel it has limited impact and also encourages resentment and defensiveness, even amongst those who have not entered into workplace intimacy due to the potential encroachment into their private lives. The predominant view is that intimacy is a sensitive human issue that cannot, and should not, be prescribed for.

The cameo of the Australian dentist (Case 25) and his Sydney practice was read by an English colleague who stated, 'I thought someone from my London practice wrote this until I noticed the word "Aussie" in the title!' Proximity, leading to close and intimate working relationships, is presented as a norm for dentists the world over. In parallel with the findings of this survey and the supporting literature review, proximity leads to close working relations, which in turn, induces more intensive emotional intimacy. However, unlike some of the conclusions reached, the Australian dentist considers that close, positive, supportive and emotional intimate working relationships can act as a brake on physical intimacy. Each individual recognises that this fine team balance can be easily upset should two or more of the parties become physically involved and thus upset the levels of trust that already exist. However, as highlighted in so many of the cases in this report, it is only a small step to take to turn emotional into physical intimacy. The Australian dentist in his closing words, highlights that the emotionally charged atmosphere of a dental practice is a worldwide phenomenon and

Case 25   Dentistry: Aussie Style

Consider working hip to hip, nose to nose, with only centimetres separating you with your surgical assistant staff member for 8 to 10 hours a day, 5 days a week, treating patients under often stressful circumstances, often finishing late into the evening! In fact, consider the total staff of 6–8 people, all generally young and attractive, working together in a 'team' environment, in an area of little over 110 square metres, needing to interrelate and communicate closely all day long, day after day, week after week, year after year. Consider every moment of your day booked to the minute, as well as after hours professional and social commitments being controlled and orchestrated by your practise manager! Let's not forget, that this same 'team' shares every high and low of your day as well as the financial health and well-being of your practise and your 'other' life!

Is this a good recipe for intimacy? ... I think so! ... I know, in my life, of no other occupation or profession where one works in such a physical and emotionally intimate environment. There are no secrets, ... we each share each others highs and lows, in both at work, and to a lesser, but very real extent, our outside life as well. The stresses of our daily work are very real ... yes, we run a modern dental specialist practise! Our work is highly creative and challenging, but nevertheless, often very stressful in both a procedural and time context.

I have two wives! One at home who runs our family and home, and the 'other' that runs my practice and the majority of my life! In fact my 'second' wife controls and runs more of my life than my real wife!

The dental practice has the potential to be a hot bed of intimacy and infidelity! Many a colleague who has run off, or had affairs with their nurse or practise manager, often because they share so much of each day together, and, from the dentists perspective at least, the staff member understands his stresses and successes so much better. It is easy to conclude simply that the staff member may be young and attractive and that this is the primary causative reason for the relationship, but I don't feel this to be the case.

Intimacy comes from sharing, understanding and respect, and in this context, the dental work environment has the real potential for intimacy at many levels. My team is very intimate ... not physically, but we all share very closely ... it is a fine line that many work environments must always be challenged by ... in a way our 'group' intimacy protects us (I hope!) in that this closeness and sharing is not undertaken with only a 'special' person, but in our case by all of us ... we respect and cherish our team, and hopefully this will never be challenged by the improbables and conflicts that can eventuate when the line is crossed!

So, when you are next in need of dental treatment, have a close look around ... You never know what may be going on in this special and unique environment!

Dental Consultant, Private Practice, Sydney, Australia

likely to continue as such. The question remains, how much of this applies to us all?

In responding to the question raised by the Australian dentist, we again refer to the literature review, which examined intimacy and sexuality and its place in society over the ages. In so doing, three distinct periods concerning home, life and work are identified,

- Agrarian societies, where working in the field took place close to home.
- Industrial societies, whereby work and home were, and are, separate.
- Information societies, whereby the distinction between work, home and personal conduct are becoming more integrated or more blurred (depends from which view point).

Thus, Figure 4.1 highlights that the current societal reconstruction (changes of norms taking place in our in society) from an industrialised to an information society, is likely to induce new structural conditions that are equally likely to encourage greater emotional intimacy, which (and has been shown in this survey) encourages physically intimate behaviour. The thesis being put forward is that particular societal pressures will increasingly become a more potent force on

SOCIETAL RECONSTRUCTION

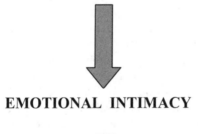

EMOTIONAL INTIMACY

INTIMATE BEHAVIOUR

Figure 4.1   Intimacy

the behaviour of individuals. Ultimately, intimacy occurrence in the workplace will be the choice made by each person. Nevertheless, with working longer, working closer and home and work life becoming blurred, intimacy is likely to be on the rise!

The prevailing attitudes and structure of each home, enterprise, government agency and even nation, will increasingly have a powerful impact on how people behave, with the final choice left to them (Marx, 1977; Near *et al*, 1980; Zadeck, 1992; Zerubavel, 1993).

Within such emerging societal forces, the perceived separation and/or linkage between home and work and consequent behaviours varies widely. For some, a clear and active separation between work and non-work domains exists in their lives, whilst for others these two critical aspects of life are intermeshed. At the one end of the spectrum, some people seek clear separation between work and non-work circumstances and, as such, adopt different behaviours for each domain. At the other end are individuals who see few delineations between home and work and can switch from one 'mindset' to another allowing work activities and behaviour to be undertaken in the non-work environment and *vice versa* (Nippert-Eng, 1996).

Further, within our emerging information society, which encourages a breaking down of boundaries, the needs of each individual vary considerably. Each person applies their own idiosyncratic interpretation concerning how to conduct their life (Nippert-Eng, 1996). They create and maintain boundaries around these critical home/work domains as a means of simplifying and/or creating order in a complex environment (Zerubavel, 1993). The demand of the information society is to 'add value' through information, ideas and intelligence. The 'three I' economy nurtures flexibility in working arrangements to an extent not previously experienced on such a mass scale. Traditionally, organisations with a genuine 24 hour, seven day a week (24/7) work ethic, such as the military, the medical profession and the police, were also rigid in exercising differentiation between work and leisure disciplines (Boyd, 1997), which new entrants to the 24/7 work ethic do not experience or need to have provided as guideline. There has always been tension, particularly in industrial societies, between work, family and leisure, and now more so in an information economy where work places constraint on the amount and quality of people's discretionary time (Kakabadse *et al*, 2003). Living in electronic 'real time' causes 'time poverty' in both spheres. As highlighted, information technology facilitates a work encroachment into personal life. Increasingly, more people are working longer hours, seemingly by necessity and with little recourse to an alternative (Kakabadse, 2000). As shown by this survey, lives are 'hurried' and increasingly self-focused (Lloyd, 1998).

Thus, the level of evident intimacy in the workplace is likely to increase due to the 24/7 syndrome. Within such a context, each case is likely to be experienced as unique, dependent on each person's needs, their level of maturity, as well as organisational and societal contexts in which they find themselves. Expressed below are the concerns of how some of the survey respondents view their present lives leading into the future.

Other relationships are driven by the challenges individuals face in their roles and their need for nurturing strong, supportive partnership interactions. Some, captured by the comments of the two clergy (Cases 29 and 30), view what has happened in the past and what is happening now, as likely to continue into the future.

Equally, a relationship can be, and may well be, driven by utilitarian self-interest, where the focus of one or both parties is on individual gain rather than on the other person or the relationship (Case 31).

Case 26   I Am a People's Person

I work through personal relationships. Relationships are important to me. I am a people's person. I have to have personal relationships with people I work with. I need to know them. Sometimes it happens that we cross the invisible boundary. It depends how I respond to the needs of others as well as my own. Having said that, it's easier 'getting personal' with some people than with others. I had three long lasting relationships at work of which two ended in a marriage. Because I used to work for traditional firms, I ended up with a price – a relationship but lost the job! Such a pattern for me may well continue.

Male Marketing Director, Multinational Corporation

Case 27   When Realised?

Because of the nature of the work and our roles, it is an asset to be like-minded on a lot of things. We are senior equity partners and relationships are important. We have been working closely for some time and then one day we both realised that we provide a focus for each other's life. Perhaps we realised it much earlier but were both afraid to admit it as other people close to us may be hurt. I can see others in my profession being in a similar circumstance.

Female Senior Partner, Legal Firm

Case 28   Sharing

It just happened that we started working together here 10 years ago and the relationship just evolved. After two mergers we became the only two senior people from the old company. One of the key things that has been import-ant for the development of our intimacy is the extreme nature of the work – changing technology and the business. That required quite close relations and working together. We shared the same challenges and issues and we started sharing a lot with one another about how we were feeling and dealing with these issues. Consequently, the relationship gained high value for both of us, from information exchange to alliance to mutual support. Now, we have a very intimate relationship that perhaps some would not approve of, considering that she has a partner.

Male IT Director, Financial Services

Case 29   Do Not Expect a Lot of Change

Depending on their denomination, people who seek a relationship with God see the clergy as their guide or intermediary, and as such, rightly expect an exemplary standard of behaviour in every way, and in particular, sexual behaviour. I think that the majority of clergy, irrespective of their denom-ination, live up to these expectations and many exceed them. Un-fortunately, and the sad truth is, that for whatever reason, there are clergy whose actions fill up newspaper pages as they fall short of any standard of decent human behaviour. Saying that, I do not think that inappropriate sexual behaviour is on the increase amongst clergy, whether between them-selves or with their parishioners. I think that these unfortunate incidents are made more public through the media and/or the civil courts, whilst in the past these incidents were the privy of the particular religious order.

Catholic Priest

As highlighted, some of the survey respondents report that the work/home interface and blurring of boundaries is an uncomfortable development. 'Quality time', for a considerable number of the survey respondents, means not bringing work home. However, for many, the demands and pressures of the job do not go away and so to accom-modate a partner's need for home life and 'quality time', the paradox is that a considerable number of executives and consultants spend more time at work so as not to bring work home. The 'honey pot' trap out-lined in Case 31 was of a senior manager whose wife held a clear view of what should be done at work and how life should be conducted at home. His desire was to take work home so as to complete his assign-ments within more comfortable surroundings. He did not share his

Case 30   *The Cross I Bear*

Religious sexual segregation is rather a modern phenomenon as theological scholarship shows that during the early Judo-Christianity period, sex was conceived as transcendent in the divine reality and therefore a person of either sex was able to make a spiritual journey beyond gender. We see things slowly changing through the ordinations of women and individuals with gender reassignment. Yet, despite such developments, what is appropriate or inappropriate sexual behaviour for clergy varies widely across religious orders and cultures. Feelings of love, intimacy, sexuality and procreation are fundamental in all human beings and they should be rightly acknowledged. Being a member of clergy does not protect one from human vulnerabilities as much as being a doctor does not prevent one from falling ill. Reflecting on my own early experience, I can say that on one particular occasion, it took a lot of prayers, contemplation and even external counselling to overcome my feelings of desire for a parishioner, which I and others deemed inappropriate for a person in my position. Could such desires re-emerge in the future? – the answer is yes. I am particularly conscious of such emotions, yes, particularly as I am married.

Male Methodist Preacher

Case 31   *Trapping Your Boss*

He was well known in the organisation and industry. He was my boss and a challenge that I had to conquer. I did not know at the time whether he went to public school, had been an altar boy or just had a strict upbringing, but he was socially shy and both emotionally and sexually repressed. This was visible in his interactions with all female colleagues. I also knew that he was married and that his wife controlled the relationship. I saw them at one of the organisational social events and observed their behaviours. It was very telling. He was attractive and considerably older than me. I am bubbly, culturally different and was new to the organisation, which is highly entrepreneurial – a swim or sink culture. I knew that if I got him on my side I could be assured of survival. But this was a challenge that required time, engagement and research. Through others I found out all his like and dislikes, from food and drinks to cars and golf. Then, during business lunches, I started ordering food and drink that I know he likes. I also talked about things that he had an interest in and eventually he noticed that we had the same tastes and similar interests. One day, after a big company event, when everyone, at midnight, drifted to their rooms and the two of us were still emptying pints of his favourite beer, he touched my hand. It was a brief moment and he blushed which was very visible as fear on his face. Then he got up and said it was getting late. He was embarrassed and I knew that he was mine if I wanted. I wanted to be sure so I waited for the next opportunity, which did not take long. Now people talk about us and some think that it is only platonic. Others suspect but no one knows. If I were to leave here, to be honest, I am likely to do the same somewhere else.

Female Consultant, Large International Consulting Firm

wife's philosophy and found it ever more a challenge to respond to her demand for home/work life separation. He all too easily fell into the category of 'my spouse does not understand me'!

The survey results also indicate that a likely growing reality is one of greater intimacy at work, not because individuals do not have a sense of 'appropriate decorum', but more because they are structurally and implicitly encouraged to enter into greater intimacy. The social circumstances in which intimacy is encouraged, where boy meets girl, are identified as occurring in the workplace with greater frequency.

The emerging challenge from this survey for managers in private and public sector organisations is, 'What are you going to do when work is also an opportunity for the pursuit of personal intimacy?'. Managers may, or many not, know what to do when the intimacy of others is drawn to their attention (Case 33) but the same challenge equally applies to all other employees (Case 32).

With the likelihood of intimacy at work being on the increase and with such a diversity of views concerning the nature and place of intimacy in the working environment, at least management should openly consider whether addressing intimacy concerns is becoming more a part

---

Case 32   Overstep The Mark And It All Goes Wrong

When I think about my relationships over the years, what probably underlies them all, and I am talking both in terms of attraction to men and friendships with women, is an inability on my part to recognise their signals unless they are made fairly explicitly. In work situations this is, of course, particularly problematic, as signals are likely to be subtler or even Machiavellian in nature.

This 'disability' on my part has caused me problems in the past. As a social and fairly extroverted person I have, on occasion, been propositioned by men at work with whom I have enjoyed what I consider to be a good platonic relationship. Looking back, if I had been able to anticipate their advances I would probably have been able to deal with them better. Instead I have found myself employing avoidance tactics, feeling very guilty and even, on one occasion, bizarrely dating a man simply because, as a friend, I couldn't bring myself to let him down. Certainly, in terms of work relationships, post my realisation of their feeling, I have found it very difficult and embarrassing to deal with these individuals which may certainly have affected my productivity. However, despite my reservations, I think that the sexual tension which is present when you are not sure of someone else's feelings can keep work interesting and fun, lead to heightened creativity and team building – until someone oversteps the mark and it all goes wrong!

Female Academic

of their work load. Knowing when to act, when not to act, and then what to do, is fraught with challenge and misinterpretation. If nothing else, managers should not be left exposed and vulnerable and with little guidance on how to respond. The survey results emphasise the need for managers to better understand the nature and conduct of personal relationships at work, as is so clearly outlined in Case 33.

The message emerging from this survey is do not leave your managers to cope on their own. Understand the intricate nature of intimacy in the workplace, talk about it and construct a view on what appropriate workplace behaviour means for you and your organisation, bearing in mind that this survey emphasises the idiosyncratic, almost unique nature of intimacy occurrences If nothing else, at least form a view as to what is the problem that requires intervention.

It was not our intention as authors of this report to be judgemental or to state what should be done (or not) over workplace intimacy encounters. What so clearly emerges from this study is that no one can really tell you, the manager, or you the individual, what you should or should not do.

Introducing more policies is unlikely to facilitate better quality working relationships, or discourage people from pursuing physical intimacy in the workplace or even reduce the number of harassment complaints. Assisting managers to understand and thus become more skilful at addressing personal sensitivities in the workplace, is the way forward.

Case 33   It Was Left Up To Me

I was made the director in a large multi national business with functional responsibility. From various rumours within the organisation, it became clear to me that one of my direct reports, a married man in his thirties with children, was having a sexual affair with a female director report. I was confronted with a number of difficulties as how to proceed. The affair was reasonably common knowledge amongst his peer group and had also come to the attention of my fellow directors. The culture in the organisation was fairly 'ladish' and not only was there no clear guidance; there had been some earlier difficulty between an alleged affair between the HR Director and another senior executive. I was confronted with the problem of whether to do anything about this and if so why? The issues that became clear in my mind were, firstly, the impact on morale within the team and secondly, the issue of power in an affair between an individual and one of his direct reports. It was also suggested to me that a number of international business trips were perhaps unnecessary.

I chose to confront the individual and ask him whether this was true or not. He denied the involvement. Without any direct confirmation there was some difficulty. I made it clear to the individual I wasn't taking the moral stand on this but merely wished to think about the organisational implications. Nevertheless, given the denial I said that I at least wished to approve all expense claims relating to the individual with whom he was alleged to be having an affair.

All seemed well for a while until the affair clearly ended. At this stage the manager became difficult and quite distant in managing his subordinate. And she, for her part, was clearly upset and didn't know how to proceed. In the event, she decided that she wanted to resign. I decided that I had to act and called her in for a chat. Again the existence or otherwise of the affair was avoided by her. Nevertheless I indicated that I thought she was an asset to the company and if she felt unable to stay working in that particular department, I would be happy to ensure a transfer elsewhere within the organisation. Clearly the break up had been so traumatic that she still decided to go. Meanwhile the reputation of the senior manager with my board colleagues was also under strain (as was his relationship with his peer group) and so his internal professional credibility subsequently diminished.

On reflection, as senior manager, it became clear that I had to both look after the individuals as well as the organisational effectiveness and reputation. I generally did not take a moral stand on this. However, the implications for the working environment certainly made me feel that there was a need for some clear guidelines to be in place. There was also a very strong issue of power. Overall, the handling of the break up was clearly unsatisfactory. My personal view is that personal relationships are inevitable in the workplace. The complications, and in this case, potential of misuse of corporate funds, became a real problem. Whatever else may be gleaned from my experience, at least my senior management team should have discussed how we proceed in such unusual circumstances. I suspect, however, my experience is no different to so many other senior managers, it was left all up to me! I am quite tough; problem is, I know others are not!

Male Finance Director, International Company

References

Adams, A. (1992), *Bullying at Work: How to Confront and Overcome it*, Virago, London.

Al-Ghazali, I. (1978), *Ihya Ulum ud Deen*, Fazlul-Karim, M.Y., translation, Islamic Book Services India.

Anderson, C.I. and Hunsaker, P.L. (1985), 'Why there's romancing at the office and why it's everybody's problem', *Personnel*, February, pp. 57–63.

Apodaca, E. and Kleiner, B.H. (2001), 'Sexual harassment in the business environment, international', *Journal of Sociology and Social Policy*, Vol. 21, Nos. 8/9, pp. 3–13.

Arnold-Baker, C. (1995), *The Life of King George VI*, Realm of Kings Number 4, Monarchist Publication, Bishop Stortford.

Arnould, E.J. and Price, L.L. (1993), 'River Magic: Extraordinary Experience and the Extended Service Encounter', *Journal of Consumer Research*, June, Vol. 20, No. 6, pp. 24–45.

Arthur, H.B. (1984), 'Making business ethics study', *Strategic Management Journal*, Vol. 5, pp. 319–333.

Associated Press (2003), 'Episcopalians Install First Gay Bishop', November 3, http://www.newsmax.com/archives/articles/2003/11/3/50822.shtml (20.12.2003).

Baker, D.D., Terpstra, D.E. and Larntz, K. (1990), 'The influence of individual characteristics and severity of harassing behavior on reactions to sexual harassment', *Sex Roles*, Vol. 22, No. 3, pp. 305–324.

Barak, A., Pitterman, Y. and Yitzhadi, R. (1995), 'An empirical test of the role of power differential in originating sexual harassment', *Basic and Applied Social Psychology*, Vol. 17, No. 4, pp. 497–517.

BBC1 (1983), 'Parkinson quits over lovechild scandal', October 14, http://news.bbc.co.uk/onthisday/hi/dates/stories/october/14/newsid_2534000/2534614.stm

BBC News (2003), 'Gay bishop answers critics', June 20, http://news.bbc.co.uk/2/hi/uk_news/3005552.stm (20.12.2003)

Bem, S.L. (1974), 'The measurement of psychological androgyny', *Journal of Consulting and Clinical Psychology*, Vol. 42, pp. 155–162.

Bcersuna, D. (1997) *Sex in the Military: The Rules of Engagement*, Time, Vol. 149, No. 22 pp. 33–35

Biema D. van (1997), 'Wings of Desire', *Time*, Vol. 149, No. 22, pp. 33–37.

Bloom, A. (1991), *Plato: The Republic of Plato*, editor, 2nd edition, Basic Books, New York.

BNA (Bureau of National Affairs) (1988), *Corporate Affairs: Nepotism, Office Romance, and Sexual Harassment*, Washington, DC.

Bordwin, M. (1994), 'Containing Cupid's arrow', *Small Business Reports*, Vol. 19, No. 7, pp. 53–58.

Borgatta, E.F. and Borgatta, M.L. (1992) (eds), 'Love', *Encyclopaedia of Sociology*, *Vol. 3*, Macmillan Publishing, New York, pp. 1164–1167.

Bouhdiba, A. (1974), *Sexuality in Islam*, Sheridan Translation, Routledge, London.

Bowes-Sperry, L. and Tata, J. (1999), 'A multi-perspective framework of sexual harassment: Reviewing two decades of research' in Powell, G. (ed.), *Handbook of Gender and Work*, Sage, Thousand Oaks, pp. 263–280.

Bowman, C., Ward, K. and Kakabadse, A. (2002), Congruent, Divergent and Incoherent Corporate Level Strategies, *European Management Journal*, Vol. 20, No. 6, pp. 671–679.

Boyd, F. (1997), 'The Puppet on the String', *Management Services*, Vol. 41, No. 1, January, pp. 38–39.

Branner, O.C., Tomkiewicz, J. and Schein, V. (1989), 'The relationship between sex-role stereotypes and requisite management characteristics revisited', *Academy of Management Journal*, Vol. 32, pp. 662–669.

Bunting, M. (2001), 'Work is turning us into emotional pygmies', *The Guardian*, May 30, p. 7.

Burrell, G. (1984), 'Sex and Organisational Analysis', *Organisation Studies*, Vol. 5, No. 1, pp. 97–118.

Burrke, R. (1994), 'Women on corporate boards of directors: forces for change', *Woman in Management Review*, Vol. 10, No. 3, pp. 16–20.

Business Week (1984), 'Audits and Surveys', August 18, p. 17.

Byrne, D. and Neuman, J.H. (1992), 'The implications of attraction research for organisational issues' in Kelley, K. (ed.) *Issues, theory and research in industrial/organisational psychology*, Elsevier Science, Amsterdam, pp. 29–70.

Cauchon, D. (1998), 'Jefferson affair no longer rumour', *US Today*, November 2, p. 3A.

Cavanagh, G.F., Moberg, D.J. and Valesquez, M. (1981), 'The ethics of organisational politics', *The Academy of Management Review*, Vol. 6, No. 3, pp. 363–374.

Chomsky, N. (2000), *Rogue State*, Pluto Press, London.

Clawson, J.G. and Kram, K.E. (1984), 'Managing cross-gender mentoring', *Business Horizon*, Vol. 27, No. 3, pp. 22–32.

Clawson, J.G. and Kram, K.E. (1984), 'Managing cross-gender mentoring', *Business Horizons*, May–June, pp. 22–32.

Clergy Disciplinary Measure (2003), *Clergy Disciplinary Measure*, No. 3, HMSO, The Stationary Office Ltd, London.

Cleugh, J. (1963), *Love Locked Out*, Hamlyn, London.

Collier, R. (1995), *Combating Sexual Harassment in the Workplace*, Open University Press, London.

Collins, E.G.C. (1983a), 'Managers and lovers', *Harvard Business Review*, September–October, pp. 142–153.

Collins, N.W. (1983b), *Professional Women and Their Mentors*, Prentice-Hall, Englewood Cliffs.

Crain, K.A. and Heischmidt, K.A. (1995), 'Implementing business ethics: sexual harassment', *Journal of Business Ethics*, April, Vol. 14, No. 4, pp. 299–309.

Cropper, C.M. (1997), 'That unwritten code against fraternisation: Companies prefer not to ask or tell', *New York Times*, October 26, p. 3:14.

Croteau, J.M. (1996), 'Research on the work experiences of lesbians, gay, and bisexual people: An integrative review of methodology and findings', *Journal of Vocational Behaviour*, Vol. 58, No. 2, pp. 195–209.

Currie, E. (2002), *Edwina Currie: Diaries 1987–1992*, Little, Brown, London.

CWN (2003), 'Scottish Bishop Apologises To church, Says He Will Marry', http://www.cwnews.com/news/viewstory.cfm?recnum=2531

Day, N.E. and Schoenrade, P. (1997), 'Staying in the closet versus coming out: relationships between communication about sexual orientation and work attitude', *Personnel Psychology*, Spring, Vol. 50, No. 1, pp. 1467–163.

DDI (Development Dimension International) (1998), Employees Speak Out on Job Training: Findings of a New Nationwide Study, DDI-Gallup-TRAINING Study, http://www.ddiworld.com/ (7 September 2003), reported in: HR Gateway (2003), 'Managers on "fault line" of skills and poor work-life balance', Editorial, 18 September, p. 1.

Deaux, K. (1985), 'Sex and Gender', *Annual Review of Psychology*, Annual Reviews Inc., pp. 49–81.

Demisch, H. (1977), *Die Sphinx, Geschichte ihrer Darstelung von den Anfangen bis zur Gegenwart*, Verag Urachhaus Johannes M. Mayer, Stuttgart.

de Rossa, P. and Murphy, A.L. (1993), *Forbidden Fruit: The True Story of my secret love affair with Ireland's most powerful Bishop*, Little Brown, Boston.

Devine, I. and Markiewicz, D. (1990), 'Cross-sex relationships at work and the impact of gender stereotypes', *Journal of Business Ethics*, Vol. 9, No. 3, pp. 333–338.

Dillard, J.P. (1987), 'Close relationships at work: Perceptions of the motives and performance of relational participants', *Journal of Social and Personal Relationships*, Vol. 4, No. 2, pp. 179–193.

Dillard, J.P. and Broetzmann, S.M. (1989), 'Romantic relationships at work: Perceived changes in job-rated behaviour as a function of participant's motive, partner's motive and gender', *Journal of Applied Social Psychology*, Vol. 19, No. 2, pp. 93–110.

Dillard, J.P. and Miller, K.I. (1988), 'Intimate relationships in task environment', in Duck, S.W. (ed.), *Handbook of Personal Relationships*, Wiley, New York, pp. 449–465.

Dillard, J.P. and Witteman, H. (1985), 'Romantic relationships at work: Organisational and personal influence', *Human Communication Search*, Vol. 12, No. 1, Fall, pp. 99–116.

Driscoll, M. (1998), 'Romance? They're working on it', *The Sunday Times*, March 22, p. 9.

DTI (Department of Trade and Industry) (2002), 'UK Workers Struggle To Balance Work and Quality Of Life As Long Hours and Stress Take Hold', *Report*, Department of Trade and Industry's (DTI) Work-Life Balance Campaign and Management Today, August, 30, http://www.dti.gov.uk/work-lifebalance/press300802.html (29 May 2003).

DTI (Department of Trade and Industry) and HM Treasury (2003), 'Balancing Work and Family Life: Enhancing Choice and Support for Parents', January.

DTS-UT (Department of Translation Studies, University of Tampere) (2000), 'Guide to Recent U.S. "Generations"' *United States Popular Culture Reference File*, Department of Translation Studies, University of Tampere, http://www.uta.fi/FAST/US7/REF/genguide.html (20 May 2003).

Ekman, P. (1992), 'An argument of the basic emotion', *Cognition and Emotion*, Vol. 6, No. 1, pp. 171–189

Elder, G. (1969), 'Appearance and education in marriage mobility', *American Social Review*, Vol. 34, No. 4, pp. 519–533.

Elliott, M. and Dickey, C. (1994), 'Body Politics: Population Wars', *The Bulletin*, September, pp. 56–58.

Ely, R. (1995), 'The power of demography: women's social constructions of gender identity at work', *Academy of Management Journal*, Vol. 38, No. 4, pp. 589–63.

Epstein, S. (1994), 'Integration of the Cognitive and Psychodynamic Unconscious', *American Psychologist*, Vol. 44, No. 1.

Erasmus of Rotterdam (1971), *In Prise of Folly*, translated by Radice, E., Penguin, London.

European Commission (EC) (1991), *European Commission Code on the Dignity of Women and Men at Work*, European Commission Code of Practice.

Farrell, S. (1998), 'Colonel bombarded ex-lover with sex calls', *The Times*, April 1, pp. 1, 3.

Faure, B. (1998), *The Red Thread: Buddhist Approaches to Sexuality*, Princeton University Press, Princeton.

Field, T. (1997), *Tim Field's workplace bullying home page*, http://www.successunlimited.co.uk.

Fisher, A.B. (1994), 'Getting Comfortable with Couples in the workplace', *Fortune*, Vol. 130, No. 7, October, pp. 70–75.

Fitt, L.W. and Newton, D.A. (1981), 'When the mentor is a man and the protégé a woman', *Harvard Business Review*, March–April, Vol. 59, No. 2, pp. 56–60.

Fitzgerald, L.F. and Shullman, S.L. (1993), 'Sexual harassment: a research analysis and agenda for the 1990s', *Journal of Vocational Behaviour*, Vol. 42, pp. 5–7.

Fleming, J.E. (1985), 'A suggested approach to linking decision styles with business ethics', *Journal of Business Ethics*, Vol. 4, pp. 137–144.

Ford, R.C. and McLaughlin, F.S. (1987), 'Should Cupid come to the workplace? An ASPA survey', *Personnel Administrator*, Vol. 32, No. 10, pp. 100–110.

Forsne, C. (1998), *François*, Points, Paris.

Foucault, M. (1979), *Discipline and Punishment*, Vintage, New York.

Fradrich, J. and Ferrell, O.C. (1992), 'Cognitive consistency of marketing managers in ethical situations', *Journal of the Academy of Marketing Science*, Summer, Vol. 20, pp. 245–252.

Francke, L.B. (1997), *Ground Zero: The gender war in the military*, Simon and Schuster, New York.

Freud, S. (1927), *The Psychopathology of Everyday Life*, Hogarth Press, London.

Friskopp, A. and Silvestein, S. (1995), *Straight job, gay lives: Gay and lesbian professionals, the Harvard Business School and American workplace*, Scribner, New York.

Gafini, M.M. (2003), 'On the erotic and the ethical', *Tikkun*, March–April, Vol. 18, No. 2, pp. 33–54.

Gaster, T.H. (1962), 'Cherubim and Seraphim', in George, A. (ed.), *The Interpreter's Dictionary of the Bible*, Abingdon Press, Nashville, Vol. 1, pp. 131–132.

Gelfand, M.J., Fitzgerald, L.F. and Drasgow, F. (1995), 'The structure of sexual harassment: A confirmatory analysis across cultures and settings', *Journal of Vocational Behavior*, Vol. 47, No. 2, pp. 164–177.

Gibbs, N. (1997), 'Sex in the military: The airforce's star female pilot finds herself enmeshed in a tale full of passion and lies', *Time*, Vol. 149, No. 22, pp. 33–35.

Gibbs, N. (1998), 'The paradox of prosperity', *Time*, No. 1, January 5, pp. 49–50.

Gilligan, C. (1977), In a Different Voice: Women's Conception of Self and of Morality', *Harvard Educational Review*, Vol. 47, No. 4, pp. 481–517.

Gilligan, C. (1982), *In a Different Voice: Psychological Theory and Women's Development*, Harvard University Press, Cambridge.

Giovanni, J.D. (1998), 'Olympic Flame', *The Times Magazine*, January 24, pp. 36–41.

Global Sex Survey (1998), 'Sexual Behaviors' *Survey Report*, Durex Global Sex Survey, http://www.durex.com/uk/sexsurvey/ (15 May 2003)

Glover, J., Fielding, J. and Smeaton, D. (1996), 'What happens to women and men with SET degrees?', *Labour Market Trends*, Vol. 104, No. 2, pp. 63–67.

Glover, S. (1998), 'Anglo-Saxon Adultery', *The Daily Telegraph*, January 30, p. 26.

Goleman, D. (1996), *Emotional Intelligence: Why it can matter more than IQ*, Bloomsbury, London.

Gruber, J.E. (1992), 'A typology of personal and environment sexual harassment: research and policy implications for the 1990s', *Sex Roles*, Vol. 26, Nos. 11/12, pp. 447–64.

Gutek, B.A. (1985), *Sex and the Workplace*, Jossey-Bass, San Francisco.

Gutek, B.A. (1996), 'Sexuality in the workplace: Key issues in social research and organisational practice', in Hearn, J., Tancred-Sheriff, P. and Burrell, G. (eds), *The Sexuality of Organisation*, Sage, London, pp. 56–70.

Hall, M. (1996), 'Private experience in the public domain: Lesbians in organisations', in Hearn, J., Tancred-Sheriff, P. and Burrell, G. (eds), *The Sexuality of Organisation*, Sage, London, pp. 125–138.

Ham, H. (2003), 'Marie Sklodowska Curie: The Woman Who Opened The Nuclear Age', *21st Century, Science and Technology Magazine*, Winter, pp. 30–68.

Hearn, J. and Parkin, P.W. (1987), *"Sex" at "Work": The Power and Paradox of Organisational Sexuality*, St Martin's, New York.

Helmrich, R.L., Spence, J.T. and Gibson, R.H. (1982), 'Sex role attitudes: 1972–1980', *Personality and Social Psychology Bulletin*, Vol. 8, pp. 656–663.

Hill, R.P. (2002), 'Managing across generations in the 21st century: Important lessons from the ivory trenches', *Journal of Management Inquiry*, Vol. 11, No. 1, pp. 60–66.

HR Gateway (2003), 'Editorial: Managers on "fault line" of skills and poor work-life balance', http://www.hrgateway.co.uk/viewnewsdetail.asp?uniquenumber=2195&loginstatus=(18.09.2003).

Hunt, M. (1959), *The National History of Love*, Alfred A. Knopf, New York.

Ibarra, H. (1993), 'Personal networks of women and minorities in management: a conceptual framework', *Academy of Management Review*, Vol. 18, No. 1, pp. 56–87.

IPD (Institute of Personnel and Development) (1997), *Key Facts: Harassment at Work*, Institute of Personnel and Development, London, May.

Irish Examiner (2000), 'Debate on celibacy a healthy step for Church', http://archives.tcm.ie/rishexaminer/2000/05/03/current/Opinion_text.htm (20.12.2003)

Johnston, P. (1997), 'Women still locked out of the boardroom', *The Weekly Telegraph*, No. 285, p. 42.

Jones, B. (1972), 'Sex in the Office', *National Times*, 12 June, p. 7.

Jones, T.M. (1991), 'Ethical decision making by individual in organisations: An issue-contingent model', *Academy of Management Review*, Vol. 16, No. 4, pp. 366–395.

Kakabadse, A. (2000), 'From individual to team to cadre: tracking leadership for the third millennium', *Strategic Change*, Vol. 9, No. 1, pp. 5–16.

Kakabadse, A. and Kakabadse, N. (1999), *Essence of Leadership*, International Thomson, London.

Kakabadse, N. and Kakabadse, A. (2004), 'Discretionary Leadership: From Control/Co-ordination to Value Co-creation through Polylogue', in Cooper C. (ed.), *The 21st Century Manager*, Oxford University Press.

Kakabadse, N., Kakabadse, A. and Kouzmin, A. (2003), 'Reviewing the Knowledge Management Literature: Towards a Taxonomy', *Journal of Knowledge Management*, Vol. 7, No. 4, pp. 75–91.

Keegan, J. (1988), *'The Mask of Command'* , Penguin Books, Hammondsworth.

Kemper, T. (1988), 'Love and like and love and love', in Franks, D. (ed.) *The Sociology of Emotions*, JAI Press, Greenwich.

Kent, R.L. and Moss, S.E. (1994), 'Effects of sex and gender role on leader emergence', *Academy of Management Journal*, Vol. 37, No. 5, pp. 1335–1346.

Kiely, J. and Henbest, A. (2000), 'Sexual harassment at work: experiences from an oil refinery', *Women in Management Review*, Vol. 15, No. 2, pp. 42–57.

Kremer, P.D. (1998), *Should you Leave?*, Gollancz, New York.

Lasswell, M. and Lasswell, N.M. (1980), *Styles of Loving*, Doubleday, New York.

Lavie, S. (1990), *The Poetics of Military Occupation*, Berkeley: University of California Press.

Lawes, R. (1999), 'Marriage: An analysis of discourse', *British Journal of Social Psychology*, Vol. 38, No. 1, pp. 1–20.

Lifton, P.D. (1984), 'Personality correlations and sex differences in moral reasoning: A comparative approach', *Journal of Personal and Social Psychology*, Vol. 43, pp. 740–762.

Lobel, S.A., Quinn, R.E., St Clair, L. and Warfield, A. (1994), 'Love without sex: the impact of psychological intimacy between men and women at work', *Organizational Dynamics*, Vol. 23, No. 1, pp. 5–16.

Lloyd, J. (1998), 'Cheating at happy families', *The Times*, January 30, p. 20.

Maccoby, E.E. and Jacklin, C.N. (1974), *The Psychology of Sex Differences*, Stanford University Press, Stanford.

Maccoby, E.E. and Jacklin, C.N. (1980), Sex difference in aggression: A rejoinder and respires', *Child Development*, Vol. 51, pp. 964–980.

MacIntyre, B. (1998), 'French Presidents' infidelities laid bare by magazine', *The Times*, February 4, p. 13.

MacKinnon, C.A. (1979), *Sexual Harassment of Working Women*, Yale University Press, New Haven.

Mainiero, L.A. (1986), 'A review and analysis of power dynamics in organisational romances', *Academy of Management Review*, Vol. 11, No. 4, pp. 750–762.

Mainiero, L.A. (1989), *Office romance: Love, power and sex in the workplace*, Rawson Associates, New York.

Malovich, N.J. and Stake, J. (1990), 'Sexual harassment on campus: individual differences in attitudes and beliefs', *Psychology of Women Quarterly*, Vol. 14, pp. 63–82.

Marcuse, H. (1986), *One Dimensional Men*, Sphere Books, London.

Markiewicz, D., Devine, I. and Kausila, D. (2000), 'Friendships of women and men at work', *Journal of Managerial Psychology*, Vol. 15, No. 2, pp. 161–184.

Marx, K. (1977), *Selected Works*, Vols. 1–13, Vantage, New York.

McIntyre, R.P. and Capen, M.M. (1993), 'A cognitive style perspective on ethical questions', *Journal of Business Ethics*, Vol. 12, pp. 629–634.

McRea, S., Davine, F. and Lakey, J. (1991), *Woman into Science and Engineering*, Policy Studies Institute, London.

Merrill, F. (1959), *Courtship and Marriage*, Holt-Dryden, New York.

Mettinger, T.N.D. (1995), *No graven image? Israelite Aniconsim in its Ancient Near Eastern Context*, Coniectanea Biblica, Old Testament Series 42, Almqvist and Wiksell International, Stockholm.

Milmo, C. (2003), 'Three million burn out Burton abandon their high flying careers in a search for the good life', *The Independent*, December 31, p. 3.

Misheler, E.G. (1979), 'Meaning in context: is there any other kind?', *Harvard Educational Review*, Vol. 49, No. 1, pp. 1–19.

Monaghan, P. (1997), *The New Book of Goddesses & Heroines*, 3rd edition, Llewellyn Publications, New York.

Morgan, G. (1986), *Images of Organization*, Sage, London.

MSF (Manufacturing Science Finance) (1994), *Bullying at Work: Confronting the Problem*, College Hill Press, London.

MSF (Manufacturing Science Finance) (1995), *Bullying at Work: How to Tackle it. A Guide for MSF Representatives and Members*, College Hill Press, London.

Murstein, B.I. (1974), *Love, Sex and Marriage through the Ages*, Springer, New York.

Near, J.P., Price, R.W. and Hunt, R.H. (1980), 'The relationship between work and work – work domains: A review of empirical research', *Academy of Management Review*, Vol. 5, No. 4, pp. 415–429.

Nippert-Eng, C.E. (1996), *Home and work: Negotiating boundaries through everyday life, 2nd edition*, University of Chicago Press, Chicago.

Nolan, B.E. (1988), *Political Theory of Beatrice Webb*, Ams Studies in Social History, No. 7, AMS Press, New York.

Overman, S. (1998), 'When labour leads to love', *HR Focus*, Vol. 75, No. 11, p. 15.

Pajo, K., McGregor, J. and Cleland, J. (1997), 'Profiling the pioneers: women directors in NZ corporate Boards', *Women in Management Review*, Vol. 12, No. 5, pp. 174–181.

Parris, M. (1998), 'Star-crossed scandals', *The Times*, January 30, p. 20.

Peterson, J. (2002), *Sexual Revolutions: Gender and labor at the dawn of agriculture*, Altamira Press, New York.

Pierce, C.A. (1997), 'Bridging the gap between romantic relationships and sexual harassment in organisations', *Journal of Organisational Behaviour*, Vol. 18, No. 2, pp. 197–200.

Pierce, C.A. and Aguinis, H. (2001), 'A framework for investigating the link between workplace romance and sexual harassment', *Group and Organization Management*, Vol. 26, No. 6, pp. 205–229.

Pierce, C.A., Byrne, D. and Aguinis, H. (1996), 'Attraction in organisations: A model of workplace romance', *Journal of Organisational Behaviour*, Vol. 17, No. 1, pp. 5–32.

Powell, G.N. (1986a), 'What do tomorrow's mangers think about sexual intimacy in the workplace?', *Business Horizons*, Vol. 29, No. 4, pp. 30–35.

Powell, G.N. (1986b), 'Effects of sex role identity and sex on definitions of sexual harassment', *Sex Roles*, Vol. 14, No. 1, pp. 9–19.

Powell, G.N. and Butterfiled, D.A. (1979), 'The "good manger": Masculine or androgynous?', *Academy of Management Journal*, Vol. 22, pp. 395–403.

Powell, G.N and Foley, S. (1998), 'Something to talk about: Romantic relationships in organisational settings', *Journal of Management*, Vol. 24, No. 3, pp. 421–448.

Powell, G.N., Posner, B.Z. and Schmidt, W.H. (1984), 'Sex effects on managerial value systems', *Human Relations*, Vol. 37, pp. 909–921.

Pringle, R. (1996), 'Bureaucracy, rationality and sexuality: The case of secretaries', in Hearn, J., Tancred-Sheriff, P. and Burrell, G. (eds), *The Sexuality of Organisation*, Sage, London, pp. 158–177.

Quinn, R.E. (1977), 'Coping with cupid: The formation, impact and management of romantic relationships in organisation', *Administrative Science Quarterly*, Vol. 22, No. 1, pp. 30–45.

Radhakrishnan, S. (1957), *A Source Book in Indian Philosophy*, Princeton University Press, Princeton.

Ragins, B.R. (1989), 'Barriers to mentoring: the female manager's dilemma', *Human Relations*, Vol. 42, No. 1, pp. 1–23.

Romer, J. (1988), *Testament, The Bible and History*, Henry Holt and Co., New York.

Rosell, E., Barber, K. and Miller, K. (1995), 'Firefighting women and sexual harassment', *Public Personnel Management*, Autumn, Vol. 24, No. 3, pp. 339–50.

Ross, L. (1998), *And here but not here: My life with William Shawn*, Random House, New York.

Rosser, N. and Kay, W. (2000), 'New look chief sacked for being too hands-on', *Earning Standard*, May 9, p. 3.

Rubenstein, M. (1988), *The Dignity of Women at Work: A Report on the Problem of Sexual Harassment in the Member States of the European Communities*, COM V/412, 1087, Office for Official Publications of the European Communities, Luxembourg.

Rubin, G. (1984), 'Thinking sex: Notes from a radical theory of the politics of sexuality', in Vance, C.SA. (ed.) *Pleasure and Danger: Exploring Roles of Men and Women*, Routledge and Kegan Paul, Boston, pp. 267–319.

Rubin, Z. (1970), 'Measurement of romantic lover', *Journal of Personality and Social Psychology*, Vol. 16, No. 3, pp. 265–273.

Schaefer, S. and Tudor, T.R. (2001), 'Managing workplace romances', *S.A.M. Advanced Management Journal*, Vol. 66, No. 3, pp. 4–10.

Schor, J.B. (1991), *The overworked America: The unexpected decline in leisure*, Basic Books, New York.

Scott, C. (1998), 'Veil comes off the Elysee mistresses', *The Sunday Times*, February 8, p. 26.

Scrivener, H. (1998), 'Free Love' *Marrie Clare*, No. 115, March, p. 138.

Seamarks, M. and Williams, D. (1998), 'Top Wren in Navy Scandal' *Daily Mail*, February 12, pp. 1, 8–9.

Segal, L. (1987), *Is the Future Female*, Virago, London.

Selbourne, D. (1999), *Moral Evasion*, Centre for Policy Study, London.

Sharp, F.C. (1989), 'An objective study of some moral judgments', *American Journal of Psychology*, Issue 9, pp. 198–234.

SHRM (Society for Human Resource Management) (2001), 'Survey Finds Romance in Workplace', *Report*, Society for Human Resource Management, Alexandria, Virginia.

SHRM (Society for Human Resource Management) (2002), 'A fine romance, but no policies', *Survey Report*, Society for Human Resource Management, Alexandria, Virginia.

Silvam J.M. and Kleiner, B.H. (2001), 'Sexual harassment in city government', *Equal Opportunity International*, Vol. 20, Nos. 5/6/7, pp. 82–87.

Singh, V. and Vinnicombe, S. (2003), *Women Pass a Milestone: 101 Directorships on the FTSE 100 Boards, The Female FTSE Report*, Centre for Developing Women Business Leaders, Cranfield School of Management Report.

Slater, E. and Roth, M. (1970), *Clinical Psychiatry*, Bailliere, Tindall and Cassell, London.

Smalensky, E. and Kleiner, B.H. (2001), 'How to prevent sexual harassment in the workplace', *Equal Opportunity International*, Vol. 18, Nos. 2/3/4, pp. 3–7.

Sprecher, S. (1985), 'Sex differences in bases of power in dating relationships', *Sex Roles*, Vol. 12, No. 4, pp. 449–461.

Sternberg, R.J.J. (1986), 'A triangular theory of love', *Psychological Review*, Vol. 93, No. 2, pp. 119–135.

Stringer, D.M., Remick, H., Salisbury, J. and Ginorio, A.M. (1990), 'The power and reasons behind sexual harassment: an employer's guide to solutions', *Public Personnel Management*, Vol. 19, No. 1, pp. 43–52.

Summersby, K. (1976), *Past Forgetting: My Love Affair With Dwight D. Eisenhower*, Simon and Schuster, New York.

Sylvester, E. (1998), 'Army's code of conduct relaxes ban on adultery', *The Daily Telegraph*, February 20, p. 1.

Symonds, W.C. (1998), 'Sex on the job', *Business Week*, February 16, pp. 30–31.

The Economist (1998a), 'The Sex Business', February 14, Vol. 346, No. 8055, pp. 19–20.

The Economist (1998b), 'The Perils of flirtation', February 14, Vol. 346, No. 8055, pp. 49–50.

The Economist (2002), 'Kiss, tell, cringe', October, Vol. 365, No. 8293, p. 33.

The Guardian (1998), 'An office fling? Time to give it the push', February 14, pp. 2–3.

The Observer (2003), 'Too Tired for Fun and Sex', *The Observer*, Sunday, June 29, pp. 1–3. http://observer.guardian.co.uk/uk-newstory/0,6903,987105,00.html/ 22.07.03

The Sunday Times (1998), 'A wickedly tempting state of affairs: Profile – The political mistress', February 1, p. 3.

Tieger, T. (1980), 'On the biological basis of sex defences in aggression', *Child Development*, Vol. 51, pp. 943–963.

Townsend, A.M. and Luthar, H.K. (1995), 'How do men feel (male sexual harassment)?', *HRM Magazine*, May, Vol. 40, No. 5, pp. 92–6.

TUC (UK, Trades Union Congress) (2003), 'Staff forced to sign long hours opt outs', Working Life: Work-Life balance, http://www.tuc.org.uk/work_life/ tuc-7084-f0.cfm (7 September 2003).

Verkaik, R. (2004), 'Sex case vicars will be tried in secret church courts', *The Independent*, January 1, p. 4.

Warfield, A. (1987) 'Co-worker romances: Impact on the work group and on career-oriented women', *Personnel*, Vol. 64, No. 5, pp. 22–35.

Waring, E.M., Tillman, M.P., Frelick, L., Russell, L. and Weisz, G. (1980), 'Concepts of Intimacy in the General Population', *Journal of Nervous and Mental Disease*, August, Vol. 4, No. 168, pp. 471–474.

Webb, S.L. (1991), 'Step forward: sexual harassment in the workplace: what you need to know', *Mastermedia*, p. 12.

Welch, J. (1998), 'Zippergate arouses move into "libido management"', *People Management*, Vol. 4, No. 19, p. 13.

Wernik, A. (1987), 'From Voyeur to Narcissist: The Imagery of Men in Contemporary Advertising', in Kaufman, M. (ed.), *Beyond Patriarchy: Essays by Men on Pleasure, Power and Change*, Oxford University Press, Toronto, pp. 277–297.

Winstead, B.A., Derlega, V.J., Montgomery, M.J. and Pilkington, C. (1995), 'The quality of friendships at work and job-satisfaction', *Journal of Social and Personal Relationships*, Vol. 12, No. 2, pp. 199–215.

Wouk, H. (1959), *This is My God, The Jewish Way of Life*, Souvenir Press Ltd, New York.

Wright, P.H. (1985), 'The Acquaintance Description Form', in Duck, S. and Perlman, D. (eds), *Understanding Personal Relationships: An Interdisciplinary Approach*, Sage Publications, London, pp. 94–112.

Zadeck, S. (1992), 'Exploring the domain of work and family concerns', in Zadeck, S. (ed.), *Work, families and organisation*, Jossey-Bass, San Francisco, pp. 24–43.

Zerubavel, E. (1993), *The fine line: Making distinction in everyday life*, 2nd edition, The University of Chicago Press, Chicago.

Index

abstinence 17
abuse of power 27, 28
'acceptable' behaviour 114
acrimony 74
actresses 10
adultery 8, 9, 10, 12, 13; prohibited 11
affairs 8–10, 14, 85, 99; alleged 126; common knowledge amongst peer group 125; concealing 77, 78; consummated 71; family history riddled with 84; marriage ended after embarking upon 57; military 12; negative signals sent out by 79; secret 57, 76; senior management levels 83; thinking about the possibility of 88; trying to hide 78
affection 15, 55, 91; gestures of 19
affective response 32
affirmation 35
affirmative action 103
aggression 24
Aguinis, H. 40
alcohol 12
alienation 59
angels 15
anger 93
Aphrodite/Venus/Freya 15
apologies 14
'appropriate' workplace behaviour 23–5
armed forces see military personnel
Arnould, E.J. 34
arousal: physiological 31; psychological 29
Artemis/Diana 15
asexuality 21
Asherea 16
assertive/aggressive comment 91
Assyria 15
attitudes 37, 38, 58, 64, 102, 112, 114, 116; differences of 24;

historical/cultural 26; shared 94; values and 94
attraction 29, 33, 101, 124; arousal instigated by 31; mutuality of 58; physical 61, 72, 73; sexual 23, 56, 73
autonomy 53
availability 65
awkwardness 79, 81, 88

Babylonia 16
Bahir 16
barriers and consequences 37–42
Becquerel, Henri 8
Bede, The Venerable 17
beliefs 26, 37, 68
Bellingham, Lt.-Cmdr. David 12
bhagwan rajneesh (osho) groups 20
Bible 16, 17
Biema, D. van 11
births 37
bishops 18
bitterness 74, 93
blame 84, 108
'blind eye' 94
body language 58
Bokassa, Catherine 10
bonds 22, 33; deep 56; emotional, strong 31; strong friendship 98
bosses 67, 79, 81; 'baby boomer' 36
boundaries 28, 75; blurring 3; breaking down of 120; invisible 121
break-ups 49, 66, 67, 109
Britain see United Kingdom
British Airways 13
Britton, Nan 9
Brunel University 38, 41
BT (British Telecom) 13
Buck, Lady Bienvenida 12
Buddhism 25, 112; sexuality 20

bullying 12; characteristic signs of 28; clergy accused of 19
Butterfield, D.A. 24

Cabbalists 16
Canaan 15
Canada 23, 106–7
Cardinale, Claudia 10
career(s) 62, 72; damage to 116; dependency 32; disrupted 73; downsides 38; goals 54; progress frustrated 103; severely damaged 12
Cartesian thinking 25
Casey, Eamon, Bishop of Galway 18
castration 17
Catholic Church 18, 122
celibacy 18, 19
Celtic tradition 15
censure 25
Centre for Policy Studies 13
Chan/Zen tradition 20
chemistry 56, 58, 64, 72
cherubs 15–16
Child Care Centres 35
childrearing 22
Chirac, Jacques 9–10
Christianity 15, 16, 17, 20, 25; 'right or wrong' moral perspective 112
Church of England: Clergy Disciplinary Measure (2003) 19; General Synod 19
clean living 17
Cleary, Fr Michael 18
clergy 121; accused of sexual misconduct 19; gay 19; inappropriate sexual behaviour 122, 123; professional conduct 19; sexually active 18
Cleugh, J. 17
Clinton, Bill 9
closeness 56, 61, 72, 101
coaching 33, 35
Code of Hammurabi 21
coercive behaviours 20, 22
cognitive style 25
cohabitation 36
collusion 40

colour 97
commitment 29, 30, 39, 98; life long 53; marriage 13
companionship 16
company policy 42, 46, 98–110; violation of 41
compatibility: interest 67; sexual 73; value 67
complaints 40, 97, 104, 125
confidentiality 43, 86, 115
conflicts of interest 115
'Consensual Relationship Contract' 42
Consistory Courts (ecclesiastical) 19
conspiracy 50
constructive dismissal 97
consumerism 22
consummation 29, 71, 113; close relationship not involving 47; potentially damaging consequences of 59
conversation 80, 91
Cook, Robin 9
corporate culture 109
courage 12, 71–2, 73, 74, 102
courts martial 11–12
cues 55
Cupid 15
Curie, Pierre and Marie 8, 10
curiosity 87; shared sense of 56
Currie, Edwina 9

dalliances 40
damage 57; potential 116; reputational 77
Datamonitor 36
dating 72; casual 66
dating agencies 13
Deaux, K. 24
deceit 78
deception 57
decision/commitment 29, 30, 31, 32
Defence Manpower Data Centre (UK) 27
deities 15
Delta Air Lines 41
demographics 36, 43, 44–6
denial 126

deontological reasoning 25
dependencies 32
desire 29, 32, 65; succumbing to
53; *see also* sexual desire
development activities 33
Deviers-Jancour, Christine 10
Dickey, C. 18
differences 24, 26; gender 31
dignity 26
directors 45
disappointment 74
disclosure 41; superficial 39
discrimination 103
distress 48, 93
diversity 54–5, 114; high performers
who promote 103; lack of 102;
promoting 100
divine feminine/masculine 16
divorce 8, 12, 13, 16, 36, 38, 66, 72,
85, 109; counselling during 18;
family history riddled with 84;
new 60; preparing for 99;
relationship inspired 71
'down shifters' 36
drive 48
drugs 12
DTI (UK Department of Trade and
Industry) 34, 35
Dumas, Roland 10

EC (European Commission) 26
Edicts of Ashika 21
EEO (European Equal Opportunities)
policy 100
EEOC (Equal Employment
Opportunity Commission) 27
ego 32, 61
Egypt 15
Eisenhower, Dwight and Mamie 11
Ekman, P. 21
Elliott, M. 18
e-mail 51, 56, 62, 87, 88;
harassment experience through
91; ignored 93; not responding
to 89, 108; shock at 93;
unusual 92; viewed as a
seductive tool 86
emotion 31, 72; 'appropriate',
expression of 22; lack of

awareness of depth of 55;
perennial tension between reason
and 21; prime 22
emotional abuse 19
'emotional aptness' 13
emotional intimacy 47, 91;
comparable levels 68;
encouraged 111, 119; gender an
insignificant consideration
concerning of 65; greatest
incidence of 67; healthy in the
workplace 58; influential brake
on 69; marriage as a result of
74; more intensive 117; ongoing
70; positive comments made
concerning 55; summarising
experiences of 82–3; viewed as
friendship 98
emotionality 20
empathy 33
Episcopal Church 19
Erasmus, Desiderius 21
Eros 15, 16
eroticism 15; anal 18
esteem 38, 53
ethics 22, 23, 25, 57
ethnic background 28, 44, 62
exemplary behaviour 122
expectations 27, 59; cultural 31;
hopeful 67; living up to 122;
not meeting 93; expectations
social 31; unfulfilled 36–7;
unmet 74
'extraordinary' service experiences
34
extreme offences 17

Factory Act (Britain 1833) 17
falling in love 1, 60, 61, 73–4, 99,
115; deeply 112; painful and
intense experience of 56
family 22, 87; break-ups 49;
growing 62; impact of work on
35; instability in 84; unresolved
patterns of relationships emerging
in next generation 86
fantasy 20, 75, 88, 90
fate 64
favouritism 38, 95

fear 105, 107; of being discovered 69; of rejection 55, 61; of repercussion 104
feelings 22, 62; distressing 93; intense, romantic and loving 29; intentionally manipulated 90; overwhelming 101; positive 33; shared 58
feminine and masculine orders 19–20
feminists 22, 23, 71
Ferrell, O.C. 24
fertility 15
flattery 61, 88, 106
Fleming, Anna 8
flexible working 35
'flings' 74
Flinn, First-Lt. Kelly 11–12
flirtation 56
Flowers, Gennifer 9
fornication 17
Forsene, Christina 10
Foucault, Michel 17
Fradrich, J. 24
France 9–10
fraternisation 11
Freud, Sigmund 17, 22
friendships 35, 63, 69, 124; basis for 60; betraying 108; encouraged 59, 98; life-long 62; platonic 99; professional relationship can progress into 58; relatively boring 49; same-sex and opposite-sex colleagues 28; special 108; strong 48; supportive and emotionally warm 51; unusual for some people 93; virtual 88; working style element to 51
fulfilment 16, 35

Gaitskell, Hugh 8
Galway 18
Garden of Eden story 15
gay men 75–6; clergy 19
gender 28; differences 24, 31; discrimination 28; equity 22; harassment based on 27; inappropriate expectations 27; insignificant consideration

concerning intimacy 65; reassignment of 123; role perceptions 23; working environment diverse in relation to 80
General Motors 41
generation X/generation Y 36–7, 42
Gilligan, C. 24
Giscard d'Estaing, Valéry 10
Gladstone, William Ewart 8
goddesses/gods 15, 16
Goleman, D. 22
gossip 40, 57, 77, 78, 81; persistent 96–7; unwelcome 74
gratification 36; sexual 29
group sex 20
guilt 101; removed 20
Gulf War units 11

happiness 29; 'generation X' basis of 36–7
harassment 25–8, 116; emotional encounters and 105; fear factor of 105; female-male 91; good case for 93; low reported incidence of 105; *see also* sexual harassment
Harding, Air Chief Marshal Sir Peter 12
Harding, Warren 9, 14
Hare Krishna 20
harmony 19, 20
Hebrew mystics 16
Hemings, Sally 9
heroes 14
Hickok, Lorena 9
Hinduism 16, 20, 25; more liberal end of 112
home working 46
homosexual harassment 28
'honey pot' trap 122
hurt 48, 57, 101
husband and wife teams 8

IBM 13
ICM Research 34
illegitimate children 9, 10
immorality 8
in flagrante delicto 25

inappropriate physical contact   19
indulgence   14, 20
infatuated love   31
infidelity   57
inhibitions   55
inhibitors   69
initiation   56, 71
innuendoes   23
intent   26
interaction   23, 24, 25, 67;
    emotionally driven   33; frequent
    32, 33, 66; greater intimacy of   47;
    jointly or mutually desired   26;
    more restricted and less
    comfortable   39; partnership,
    strong, supportive   121;
    professional, intensive   59; sexual
    26; virtual   88
interests: compatible   67; similar
    65, 80
International Conference on
    Population and Development
    (Cairo 1994)   18
intimacy   28–37; addressing
    111–26; clergy   18; fear of the
    consequences of   38;
    international study of   43; nature
    and context   46, 47–55; nature
    and level of incidence   43;
    outcomes and impact   69–86;
    psychological   23; repercussions
    of   43; research into, considered
    taboo   21; *see also* emotional
    intimacy; physical intimacy
intolerance   109
involvement: choosing level of   68;
    direct   69–78; emotional   67,
    112; potential for   34; resentment
    and lawsuits engendered by   40;
    third party   79–86
Ishtar   15
Islam   19–20, 25
IT (information technology)
    revolution   46, 86–91
Italians   13

jealousy   11, 48, 96
Jefferson, Thomas   9
Jobert, Marlene   10

John, Canon Jeffrey   19
Johnson & Johnson   41
joint interests   48
Judaism   16, 25, 112; view of
    sexuality   19, 20
Jungian personality types   25

Keays, Sara   9
Kennedy, John F.   9
Key, Lt. Joanna   12
kindred spirit   58
King Solomon's temple   16
Kings (Book)   16
KPMG   13
Kristel, Sylvia   10

language   60
leadership positions   24
legal action   97
LeHand, Marguerite Alice ('Missy')   9
Lewinsky, Monica   9
liaisons: office   13; romantic   42;
    sexual   49, 112
liberation   20
libidinal energy   20, 21, 22
Lifton, P.D.   24
liking   29, 32, 112
limbic system   21–2
Lloyd George, David   8, 13–14
Lloyd's of London   41
Lobel, S.A.   30
logic   72
lone parent families   35
love   11, 13, 14, 40, 63, 74, 100;
    'complete'   31; different forms of
    112; magical spells   15;
    nauseatingly happy in   57;
    romantic   36; strong as ever
    102; triangular theory of   29; true
    57, 72; unrequited   61; *see also*
    falling in love
'love contract' policies   41
loyalty   12, 98, 109
lust   17, 19

magical power   15
Mahvyvna Buddhism   20
Mainiero, L.A.   32
Major, John   9

Malchut 16
male-dominated professions 27
management intervention 91–8
Marcuse, H. 21; marital strife 38
Marks and Spencer 13
marriage 8, 19, 42, 68; based on
 'social aptness' 13; births
 conceived outside 37; changed
 from commitment/family values to
 personal gratification 36;
 considerable sexual activity outside
 112; convenience 63; couples
 will be a minority in Britain 13;
 emotional/physical intimacy
 resulting in 74; ended 57, 72–3;
 former, maintaining civility for the
 sake of son 66; marriage happy
 63, 109; importance of 53;
 intimacy outside 9; *joie de vivre* of
 20; living together before 13;
 military 11; relationships which
 ended in 121; sanctity of 53;
 second or third 44; spiritual
 matter, between man and wife
 17; unhappy 62, 73, 99;
 wife-controlled 123
masculinity and femininity 24
maternity pay/leave 35, 64
May month 15
MBA (Master of Business
 Administration) degrees 24
medical profession 120
mentoring 33, 34, 59
Mercer, Lucy Page 9
Mesopotamian texts 15
Methodists 123
middle and senior management 44
mid-life transition/crisis 36, 114
military personnel 10–12, 27, 80,
 120
misconduct 11; punishment for
 17; sexual 19, 55
misinterpretation 125
mistresses 9; long-established 10;
 'paying off' 14
Mitterrand, François 9, 10
moral absolutes 20
moral judgement 28; sexually based
 25

morale 125; group/team 40, 82
morality: guardian of 15; outdated
 78
Morgan, G. 17
motives 32; primary 40
Murphy, Annie 18
mutual admiration 61

neurology 21, 22
New Zealand 23
non-fraternisation policy 41

obsession 108
office romances 13, 25–6
Ojjeh, Nahed 10
olfactory functions 21–2
'one of the boys' 50
organisational culture 51–3, 69,
 102, 116
ostracism 28, 40
overnight stays 46
pagan traditions 15, 16

palpitations 31
Papandreou, Andreas and Mimi 10
parents 35
Parkinson, Cecil, Lord 9
Parris, M. 14
passion 22, 30, 31, 32, 71
Pearce, Lt.-Cmdr. Karen 12
peers: affair common knowledge
 amongst 125; criticism from 7;
 negative reaction from 69;
 personal standing amongst 14
penance 17
personal learning 48, 57, 62, 90
personality 93; anal 17; Jungian
 types 25; similar 48
Pertemps 13
Phoenicia 15
phone calls 108; asking for a date
 96; messages not returned 89
physical intimacy 47, 68, 91; closely
 linked with sexual harassment
 104; disruptive to effective team
 working 58; fine line between
 emotional and 55; gender an
 insignificant consideration
 concerning 65; incidences of

67, 70, 103, 112; influential brake
on 69; marriage as a result of
74; migrating from emotional to
68; obtrusive and causing
disruption 95; powerful inhibitor
of 69; prime cause of 59;
response of organisation to 100;
sexual harassment and 58; sharp
distinction between harassment
and 105; summarising
experiences of 82–3; training on
how to address 115; viewed in a
positive light 111
physical violence 28
Pierce, C.A. 40
Pingeout, Anne 10
Plat, Capt. Alison 12
Plato 14, 17
platonic connections 29, 99
pleasure 16, 22; unacceptable 53
police 43, 120
politics 8–10; libidinal 23
Pople, Lt.-Col. Keith 12
Potter, Beatrice *see* Webb
Powell, G.N. 24
pregnancy 20
premarital sex 36
Price, L.L. 34
private sector organisations 43
proclivity 40, 43, 65, 68
procreation 15, 17
professional conduct 38
professionalism 77, 90
professional/technical occupations
23, 44
promises 14
promotion 23, 38, 50; prospects
unlikely to be harmed 103
propriety 55
prosecutions 11
protégés 38
proximity 32, 58, 65, 117
psychiatry 21
public knowledge 57
public service agencies 43
punitive measures/punishment 11,
17, 112

Quinn, R.E. 38

racial-based harassment 28
rape 27
rapid breathing 31
rapport 88
rationality 19, 21
reactions 88, 98; common 79,
91, 113; extreme 31;
management 91, 95, 98, 113,
114; negative 69;
reason 21
recruitment consultants 13
Regan, Gaynor 9
rejection 55, 61
relationships 13, 41, 49; covertly
conducted 7; cross-gender,
mentoring 34; discreet 91, 94;
dissolution of 40; extra-marital
109; hierarchical 32; inter-office
101; lies over 14; long-lasting
121; loving 32; low profile 49;
nature of 55–69; open and
unobtrusive 94; power-based
40; romantic 31, 37, 38, 39;
sexual 38, 40; social 23; special
88; too intense 100; virtual
87–90; war-time 11
religion 25, 28, 44, 62; sexual
segregation 123; sexuality and
14–20
re-marriage 84, 101, 109
remorse 14
repercussion 104
repressed sexuality 17–18, 123
reputation 76, 116; loss of 77
resentment 40, 76, 117
resignation 41
respect 61; loss of 38; mutual
intellectual 56
restraint 17
Rippon, Geoffrey, Lord 8
risks 37–8, 88
Robinson, V.Gene, Bishop of New
Hampshire 19
role models 73, 74, 114
romance(s): consequences of 39;
dissolved 40; drivers that foster
29; induced to go 'underground'
40; likelihood of 36; long-term
13; not recommended 67

Roosevelt, Franklin D. and Eleanor 9
Ross, Lillian 14
Rubin, G. 23
Rubin, Z. 30
rumours 96, 108

sacred places 15
satisfaction 16, 29, 39; deep 99; job 48, 54, 65
Saxons 15
scandal 7–8, 10, 11–12, 14, 55; 'needless' 18
Schor, J.B. 33
sectarian-based harassment 28
security 67
Segal, L. 22, 32
self-image 38
self-satisfaction 33
selfishness 108
sense of smell 21
'sensitive topics' 18
sensuality 15, 20
separation 74
sex roles 31
sexual abuse/assault 19, 27
sexual desire 22, 29; realisation of 23; unique, not harmful or perverted 20
sexual domination 22
sexual favours 27
sexual freedom 15
sexual harassment 3, 5, 11, 20, 22, 23; accusations of 40; affair turned into 12; company policy 42; defined 26; fine line between physical intimacy and 58; incidences of 27, 103; increased possibility of 91; not tolerated 103; of men 27; organisation's tolerance for 40; perceived 26–7; physical intimacy closely linked with 104; public relations damage 25; US policies 28
sexual health 18
sexual imagery 22
sexual preference 28
sexuality 119; international study of 43; religion and 14–20

Shakti/Kali/Durga/Bhairavi 15
sharing: similar interests and perspectives 58; time and secrets 56
Shawn, William and Cecille 14
Shechinah 16
Shiva and Shakti 16
SHRM (Society for Human Resource Management) 42
shyness 92, 123
single status 13, 68
Sklodowska, Marie *see* Curie
sociability 96
'social aptness' 13
social controls 17
social events 123; company-sponsored 66; pretending for 78
'social graces' 14
social life 59
social pressures 17
socialising 58
sorrow 108
Spaniards 13
speculation 57
sphinxes 15
'spoilt brat' dependency syndrome 37
standards 57
Staples 41
staring 96, 97
stereotypes 24, 39; reversal of 63
Sternberg, R.J.J. 29, 30, 31, 32
subliminal form 18, 21
Sufis 19
Summersbay, Kay 11
supervision 28
support 57, 95, 114, 115; appraisal 33; emotional 33, 72; informational 33; instrumental 33; mutual 13, 122; social, collegial 33
survival mentality 37
suspicions 83
sweating 31
symbols 15
symptoms 31
Syria 15

Talmud 16
Tantric tradition 20
Taoist thought 16
Tax Credits 35
teams 65, 69; building 33, 98
'Teflon' factor 13
teleology 25, 26
television soap operas 18
temperance 14, 22
temptation 53, 90
Ten Commandments 21
tension 21, 40; relieving 95;
    sexual 71, 124
termination of contracts 41
text messages 108
threat to employment 69
Tibb al-Nabawi 19
Tiferet 16
tolerance 94
touching 104, 107; deliberate 27;
    inappropriate 19; women's
    bottoms 13
training 114, 115
trauma 70
travel 46
tribunals 19
'trouble makers' 103
trust 61, 63, 81; damaged 12, 77;
    deteriorating 82; gaining 90;
    mutual 57
TUC (Trades Union Congress) 35–6

UCL (University College London)
    38, 41
Unani Medicine 19
unethical behaviour 7
United Kingdom 41; couples living
    together before they marry 37;
    female directors 23; impact of
    work on family life 35; military
    environment 12, 80; working
    hours 34, 36

United Nations 18
United States 9, 37, 41, 71;
    corporate culture 109; infidelity
    technically not illegal 11;
    military environment 11–12, 80;
    sexual harassment
    incidences/polices 27, 28
unlawful gender discrimination
    28
unwanted sexual conduct 26, 27
'unwelcome' comments 12–13
upheavals 73
urge 16

values 17, 48; compatible 67;
    deeply held 53; different 73;
    family 53; personal 68; sacred
    18; shared 94
verbal intimidation 28
villains 14
violation 25
virtues 17

Waring, E.M. 33
'weak willed' people 53–4
Webb, Sidney and Beatrice 10
'whistle blowers' 104
'wife' status 13
Wilson, Harold 14
working hours 34, 36, 98m
    120–1
wrongdoing 20, 112

Xerox 13

Yah-weh 16
Yin and Yang 16
Yod-Dalet-Ayin 16

Zigo, Marc 12
'Zippergate' 84
Zohar 16